True Fact:
In medieval times, people
believed that the position in
which a couple conceived a
child could determine the
baby's gender.

**True
In medieval Europe,
it was believed that the
position in which a couple
conceived a child could
determine the baby's gender.**

I
*really want
a boy*

If we 69
can we get
twins?

What was a popular aphrodisiac in the 16th century?

a) Ground unicorn horn
b) fresh oysters
c)Pickled frog balls
d) A potion made from tears of lovestruck poets

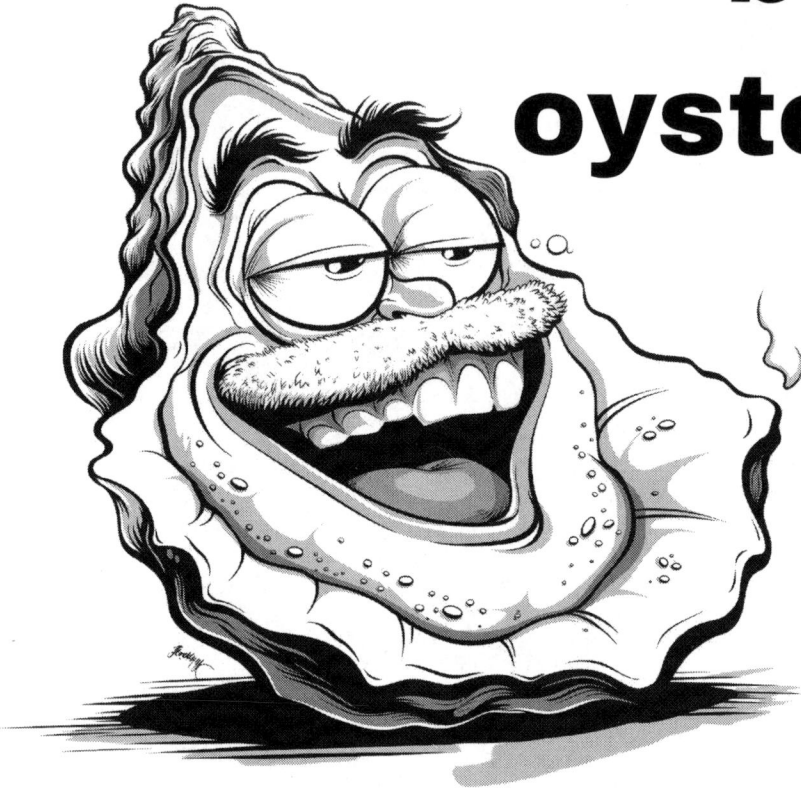

In ancient Greece
Independent prostitutes who
worked the street wore sandals
with marked soles which left an
imprint on the ground that stated
ΑΚΟΛΟΥΘΕΙ AKOLOUTHEI

Which when translated means
A-Daughter of Aphrodite
B- Me so horny
C-Me love you long time
D-Fun-Laughs-Good-times
E-Follow me

follow me

WHAT WAS THE PENALTY FOR ADULTERY IN ANCIENT ROME?

A) EXILE:

BECAUSE THE GRASS IS GREENER ON THE OTHER SIDE OF THE EMPIRE

B) DEATH BY STONING:

TALK ABOUT A ROCKY RELATIONSHIP

C) PUBLIC FLOGGING:

A LESSON IN LOVE... AND HUMILIATION

D) FORCED DIVORCE:

WHEN "IRRECONCILABLE DIFFERENCES" MEANT SOMETHING ELSE ENTIRELY

B)

GETTING STONED TO DEATH: TALK ABOUT A ROCKY RELATIONSHIP.

What was the nickname given to the brothels that operated in ancient Greece?

a) Pleasure Palaces:
Where philosophers pondered the mysteries of the universe... among other things.

b) Aphrodite's Havens:
Where Cupid's arrow shoots below the belt !

c) Lotus Beds:
Botanicals, Butts and Boobs! Oh my!

d) Houses of Ill Repute:
Where reputations were lost and found.

e) Porneia:
We deliver more happy endings than a Hallmark movie .

e) Porneia

Brothels in ancient Greece were commonly known as "porneia" or "porneion." They were establishments where sexual services were provided by prostitutes, who were referred to as "porne" or "hetaira."

What was invented first
the dildo
or
the wheel?

Upper Paleolithic art dating back 30,000 years depicts people using dildos to pleasure themselves and others. mankind invented sex toys long before the wheel

What was the original purpose
of the vibrator when it was
invented in the 19th century?

a) To mix drinks
b) To treat "hysteria" in women
c) To massage sore muscles
d) To polish shoes

To treat hysterical women

Female hysteria was a common diagnosis at the time for a wide range of symptoms, including anxiety, irritability, and sexual frustration. It was believed that these symptoms were caused by a "wandering womb" that needed to be stimulated in order to bring relief.

The first electromechanical vibrator was patented in 1880.The device was a large, cumbersome machine that was used by doctors to provide manual stimulation to women in order to induce "hysterical paroxysm" (orgasm) as a treatment for their symptoms.

In ancient Egypt, what was considered a sign of fertility and often worn as a charm?

a) A scarab
b) A cat
c) A pyramid
d) A sphinx

A Scarab

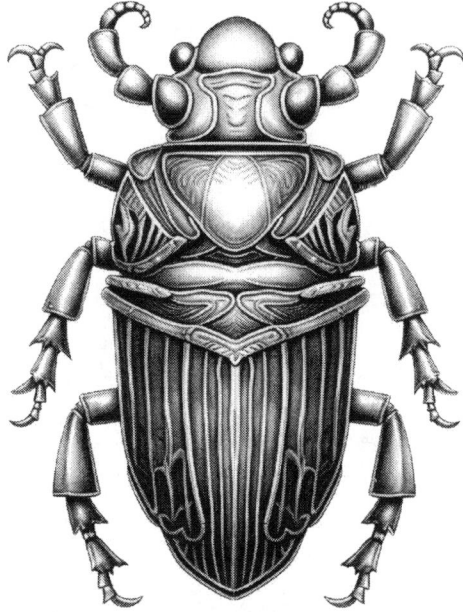

Scarabs were considered a symbol of fertility in ancient Egypt. The scarab beetle was associated with the god Khepri, who represented the rising sun and the cycle of creation and rebirth. The ancient Egyptians observed the behavior of scarab beetles rolling balls of dung, which they used as a nesting place for their eggs. This behavior was seen as a parallel to the sun rolling across the sky and the subsequent rebirth of the sun each day.

**What was the Church's
stance on sex
during the Middle Ages?**

a) "Do it for the vine!"

**b) "Only for procreation,
you heathens!"**

**c) "It's all good as long
as your married."**

d) "What's sex?"

b)
**"Only for procreation,
you heathens!"**

The word "clitoris" is

A. Greek for "divine and goddess like."

B. Latin for "hidden treasure."

C. French for "pleasure button."

D. German for "source of joy."

E. Summarian for "the tiny boatman"

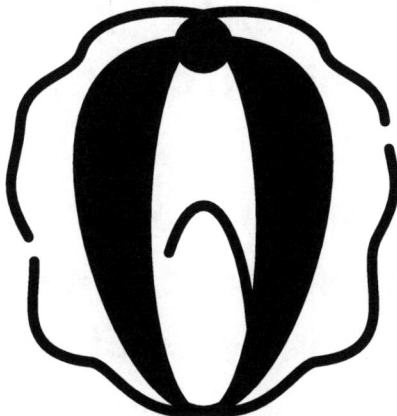

A. Greek for "divine and goddess like."

The word "clitoris" comes from the Greek word kleitoris, which can be translated as "little hill" or "to rub", hinting at some cheeky wordplay from way back when.

Which historical figure is rumored to have said,

"I may be drunk, Miss, but in the morning I will be sober and you will still be ugly"?

a) The original king of one-liners: Winston Churchill

b) Mark Twain: Proving that wit knows no bounds

c) Statesman by day, comedian by night : Benjamin Franklin

d) George Bernard Shaw: Playwright and master of the backhanded compliment

a)

Winston Churchill

He also said:
I am fond of pigs.
Dogs look up to us.
Cats look down on us.
Pigs treat us as equals.

What did the ancient Romans use as a contraceptive?

a) Olive oil
b) Silphium
c) Garlic
d) Wine
e) Tomato sauce

Silphium

A plant that is now extinct because they used it so much.

Which famous French king supposedly had dozens of illegitimate children?

a) Louis XIV
b) Louis XV
c) Louis XVI
d) Louis CK

d)
Louis XV.
Known as "Louis the Beloved," he was rumored to have fathered numerous illegitimate children during his reign, contributing to his extensive lineage.

TRUE OR FALSE

IN ANCIENT GREECE, AN AVERAGE SIZE PENIS WAS A SIGN OF INTELLIGENCE

What did ancient Chinese emperors use to enhance their sexual performance?

a) Ginseng and deer antlers
b) Tiger bone and rhino horn
c) Dragon blood and phoenix feathers
d) A scrotom plaster of rice wine and soy sauce

Ginseng and deer antlers

What was the most popular aphrodisiac in ancient Egypt?

a) Caviar
b) Cinnamon
c) Lotus flowers
d) Sandalwood
e) Mummy Dust

NOT WITH MY
MUMMY IN THE ROOM!

Lotus Flower

Which 18th-century ruler of Russia had a secret "Cabinet of Curiosities" filled with erotic art and objects?

a) Catherine the Great
b) Peter the Great
c) Ivan the Terrible
d) Boris the Bold

Catherine the Great

In the 18th century, what was the prevailing attitude towards female sexual pleasure?

a) Embraced and encouraged

b) Discouraged and frowned upon

c) Ignored and considered irrelevant

d) Celebrated as a natural aspect of life

b)

Discouraged and frowned upon, because apparently, the idea of women enjoying themselves was as scandalous as mismatched socks at a royal ball. speaking of royal balls ....

There was a prevailing belief that women's primary purpose in sexual relations was procreation, and any pursuit of personal pleasure was seen as unnecessary or even sinful. Discussions or expressions of female pleasure were considered indelicate and improper, and women were discouraged from exploring or asserting their own sexual desires.

Which historical figure was known for their scandalous love affairs?

a) Queen Mary
b) Henry VIII
c) Isaac Newton
d) Amelia Earhart

b)
Henry VIII.
His multiple marriages
and divorces
were quite a sensation.
He is tied with
Elizabeth Taylor.
Both were married and divorced
7 times.
Luckily Richard Burton
never lost his head !

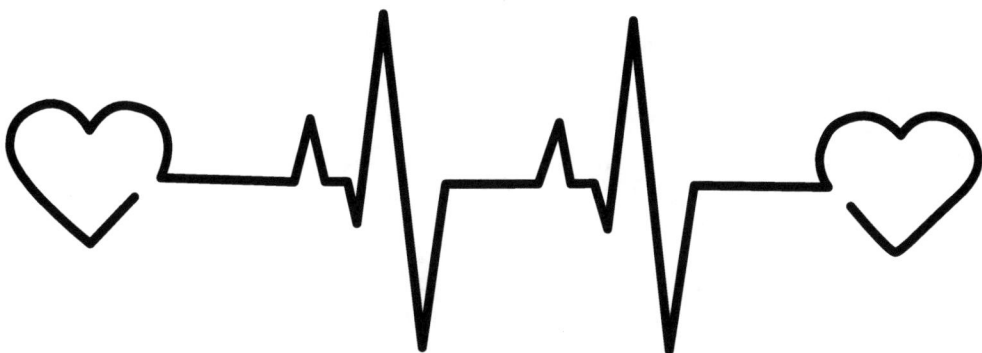

Which famous person said, "Sex relieves tension-love causes it"?

a) Charlie Chaplin
b) Plato
c) Woody Allen
d) Friedrich Nietzsche

**Woody Allen.
Not exactly ancient
history, but still a classic.**

In Medieval Europe, what was a common treatment for impotence?

a) Eating a dozen oysters

b) Riding a horse naked through a field of crops

c) Drinking a potion made from unicorn horn

d) Praying to the gods of fertility

e) Consuming spanish fly

**Spanish Fly
(which is actually
made from ground beetles)**

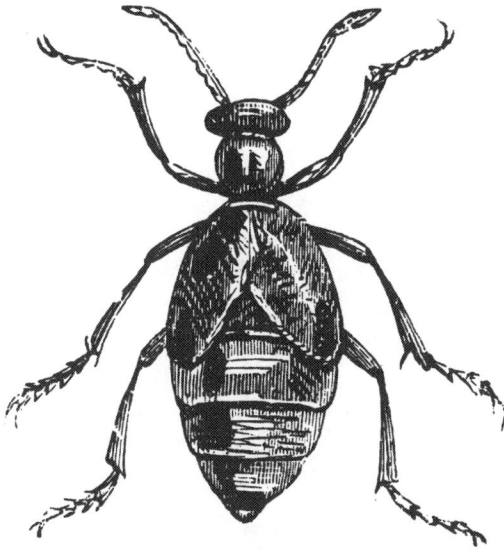

True Spanish fly is derived from dried blister beetles, from a substance they produce called cantharidin. The name of this insect is no joke – cantharidin can blister your skin upon contact!

The dried beetles would be crushed and mixed with drinks or sweets, often without the knowledge of the receiver. This was done in the hopes of promoting a warm, tingling sensation throughout the body and swelling of the genitals. However, these "warm fuzzies" were actually due to inflammation.

But here's the kicker – along with those long-lasting erections, Spanish fly was found to have some dangerous side effects, including death. The infamous Marquis de Sade discovered this in 1772 when he laced sweet aniseed balls with Spanish fly that he fed to prostitutes, who later suffered gruesome deaths.

What was the first country to legalize same-sex marriage?

a) United States
b) Canada
c) The Netherlands
d) Spain

The
Netherlands

What was the name of the first sex manual, written in India around the 2nd century?

a) The Art of Love
b) The Kama Sutra
c) The Perfumed Garden
d) The Pillow Book

The Kama Sutra

The Kama Sutra, an ancient Indian gem, is like a swanky love manual penned by the wise Vatsyayana. It's not just a playbook of steamy moves, but a love guru preaching the gospel of respect, communication, and romance. This ancient masterpiece doesn't just talk about love in the bedroom, but also dishes out wisdom on how to ace relationships with style. It's a timeless treasure chest of love tips, desire whispers, and the secret recipe for a vibrant and spicy life!

Who said:

"I don't care how old you get, a woman ought stay sexy for her husband"

A.
Jane Fonda
B.
Betty White
C.
Queen Elizabeth
D.
Tammy Faye Baker

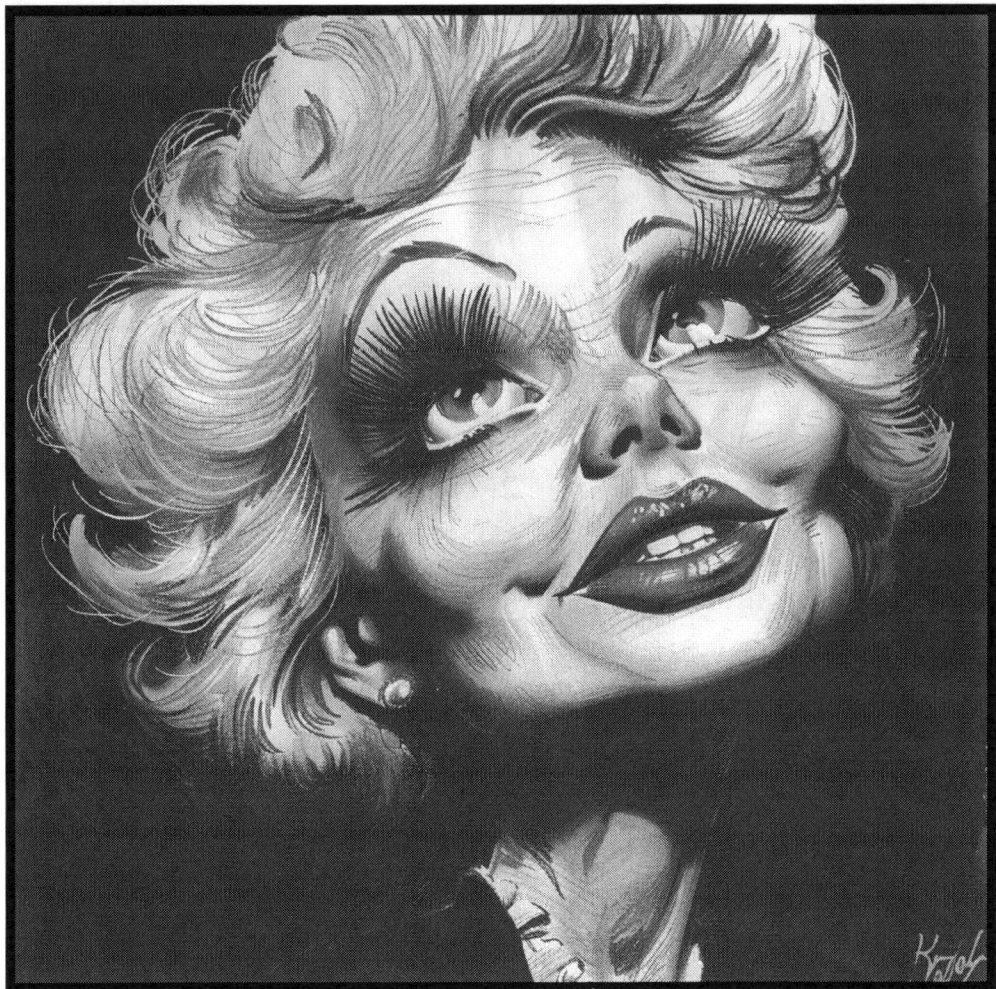

Tammy Faye Bakker

She also said:
"You don't have to be dowdy to
be a Christian."

Who said:

*"The only way to
rid yourself of temptation
is to yield to it ?"*

A. Betty White

B. Mark Twain

C. Oscar Wilde

D. Socrates

Oscar Wilde

*"Never love anyone
who treats you
like you're ordinary."*

Which quote has been attributed to both Betty White and George Carlin

If men could get pregnant, abortions would available

A.
at Jiffy Lube.

B.

at Taco Bell.

C.

at the DMV.

D.

at the bowling alley .

"If men could get pregnant, abortions would be available at Jiffy Lube."

What was the average age of marriage in the Middle Ages?

a) 13

b) 20

c) 29

d) Whenever you could grow a decent beard.

In Italy, sons traditionally lived with their fathers in cities, delaying marriage to preserve family wealth and social standing. Up north, independence and skills were valued before marriage. Craftsmen honed their craft and country boys established their own homes. Guilds influenced the age for journeyman status and marriage, allowing men to save money before committing.

What was the most common form of birth control in the Middle Ages?

a) The rhythm method
b) Coitus interruptus
c) Condoms
d) Wishing upon a star

**c)
Condoms
(made from
sheep intestines)**

What was considered the most attractive feature in a woman during the Middle Ages?

a)

A voluptuous figure

b)

A high forehead

c)

A good sense of humor

d)

The ability to churn butter

b)
A high forehead

In the past, a high forehead was considered a sign of beauty. Women and girls who did not have this feature naturally would pluck their foreheads, sometimes using hot pins to prevent regrowth, in order to achieve the desired smooth, almost baby-like appearance.

Which of the following methods was used in an insane asylum to deter masturbation?

A) Circumcision without anesthesia
B) Yogurt enemas
C) Ice baths
D) Carbolic acid to the genitals
E) A healthy breakfast of Kellog's Cornflakes
E) All of the above

E) All of the above.
Dr. Kellogg believed in a range of extreme measures, including a bland diet and vegetarianism, all with the aim of deterring masturbation. He created his now famous cornflakes to feed the inmates and keep desire at bay. All part of Dr. Kellogg's approach to promoting what he considered to be a healthy and virtuous lifestyle. No frosting on these flakes!

What legendary scientist was so passionate about math they are rumored to have never had sexual relations.

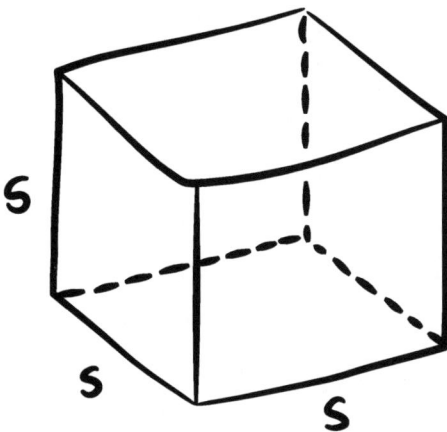

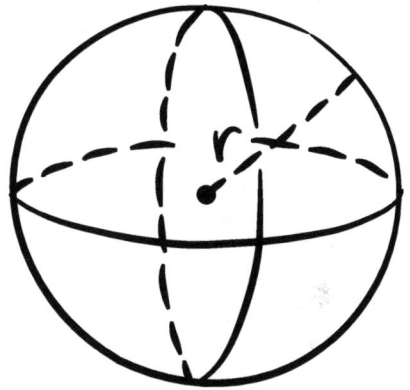

$$V = \frac{4}{3}\pi r^3$$

$$V = s^3$$

Sir Isaac Newton!

This brainiac rocked the world of math, physics, and astronomy. His claim to fame? The legendary book "Philosophiæ Naturalis Principia Mathematica" (try saying that three times fast!), where he spilled the beans on his laws of motion and gravity. Talk about setting the stage for modern science! On top of all that, Newton was big on theology and biblical studies. And hey, while rumors about his love life remain a mystery, it's clear this guy was all about work, work, work!

Who wrote the book published in 1970 <u>Human Sexual Inadequacy</u>

A

Sigmund Freud

B

Dr. Ruth Westheimer

C

Masters and Johnson

D

Sonny and Cher

Masters and Johnson
William H. Masters and Virginia E. Johnson in 1966, both published Human Sexual Response. In 1970, Human Sexual Inadequacy was published. Today, the publications are considered as classic texts.
They were a pioneering couple in the field of sex research, conducting groundbreaking studies on human sexual response and dysfunction. Their work helped to destigmatize sexual issues and paved the way for improved understanding and treatment of sexual problems.

What does "the passion of the cut sleeve" symbolize in chinese culture?

Cut-sleeve 断袖 (duàn xìu) is a euphemism that refers to male homosexual individuals and male same-sex love in Chinese culture. The term dates back to around 10 BC.

Which ancient Chinese emperor expressed such tender affection towards his male lover that this compassionate gesture became the euphemism for homosexuality in Chinese culture.

Ming Wang

Chow Fun

Al Han

P.F Chang

Sum Yung Gai

Too Wong Fu

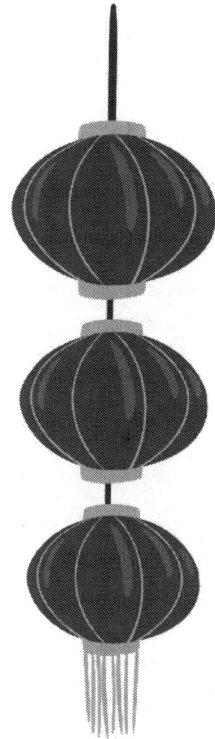

AI HAN

Emperor Ai,an openly bisexual emperor during the Han dynasty, had a well-known relationship with Dong Xian. Historically, their bond was described as that of homosexual lovers, often referred to as "the passion of the cut sleeve." This term originated from a tale where Dong fell asleep on the emperor's shoulder. When the emperor wanted to get up, he cut his sleeve rather than wake his still-sleeping lover. Courtiers were so moved by the sweetness of his act they all cut one sleeve off their Kimono's .

Though the emperor also had a wife and several concubines, one of whom was Dong's sister, records say that Dong slept in the emperor's bed, and was rewarded with hair combs and baths like any imperial consort.However, Ai's favoritism had a cost: Dong was promoted to be a military commander in a very short period, creating discontent at court.

In a massive 179-page encyclical called Veritas Splendor, John Paul II reaffirmed the church's stance on a variety of topics. What did he say no to?

A)premarital sex
B)contraception
C)homosexuality
D)abortion
E)masturbation
F)No! to all of the above.

E) No! to all of the above
Altar boys don't count

What was the ancient
Chinese belief about the
female orgasm?

a) It was a myth
b) It was necessary for
conception
c) It was a sign of
demonic possession
d) It was a cure for
headaches

b)
It was necessary for conception

What was the ancient Chinese version of a sex manual called?

a) The Art of War
b) The Book of Songs
c) The Pillow Book
d) The Yellow Emperor's Classic of Medicine

"THE YELLOW EMPEROR'S CLASSIC OF MEDICINE."
YES, THE ANCIENT CHINESE KNEW THAT A HEALTHY BODY AND A HEALTHY SEX LIFE GO HAND IN HAND! THE YELLOW EMPEROR MIGHT NOT HAVE PRESCRIBED VIAGRA, BUT HE SURE HAD SOME SAGE ADVICE FOR KEEPING THINGS IN BALANCE! ACCORDING TO HIM, MAINTAINING HARMONY IN THE BEDROOM WAS AS CRUCIAL AS IT WAS IN ANY OTHER ASPECT OF LIFE. MODERATION IS KEY – TOO MUCH OF A GOOD THING MIGHT THROW OFF YOUR YIN AND YANG FASTER THAN YOU CAN SAY "ANCIENT APHRODISIACS"!

What was the ancient Chinese belief about sex during pregnancy?

a) It was encouraged for a healthy baby

b) It was forbidden as it could harm the baby

c) It was only allowed during full moons

d) It was believed to determine the baby's gender

a)

It was encouraged for a healthy baby

TRUE OR FALSE

MARRIED PEOPLE ARE MORE LIKELY TO MASTURBATE THAN PEOPLE LIVING ALONE.

True

**Married people
are more likely
to masturbate
than people living alone.**

The fear of having, seeing, or thinking about an erection is called:

A. Rigorpeniphobia

B. Ithyphallophobia

C. Erectiphobia

D. Streptocockiphobia

E. Jr. high

ITHYPHALLOPHOBIA

Ithyphallophobia, also known as the fear of seeing an erect penis, it's a real thing, folks. So, if you have this fear, just remember to keep your eyes closed during those awkward locker room moments

Ithyphobia is the fear of touching or being touched by feathers. People may experience intense anxiety or panic when exposed to feathers .

Knismolagnia
refers to a sexual interest
or arousal derived from

A) from flatulence or farting.
B) from playing with raw fish.
C) from tickling or being tickled.
D) watching the Golden girls naked.

Tickle Fetish

Who said:
"What is the best life?
To be tickled to death "

a)lady Gaga

b) Nietzsche

c)Big Bird

d)Marie Antoinette

e) Marquis De Sade

Nietzsche

I want a little
test tickle

Centuries ago, the Muscovite palaces and courts took tickling to a whole new level by using foot tickling as a means of sexual arousal.

Eunuchs and women were employed as professional foot ticklers, honing their skills to perfection and earning prestige and good pay for their ticklish talents.

Which russian royal regularly Indulged in feet tickling?

a) Catherine the Great,
b) Anna Ivanovna,
c) Anna Leopoldovna
d) Elizaveta Petrovna
e) All of them

All of them

IHRO HOHEIT
die Prinzeßin
ANNA

Anna Leopoldovna, in particular, took foot tickling to the next level, having at least six ticklers at her beck and call.

what else did the ticklers do while they performed their tickling magic ?

A) Told bawdy stories and sang obscene ballads
B)Discussed politics and gossip
C) Served tea and cakes
D)Masturbated wildly
E) Bet on the ponies

Sang obscene ballads and told bawdy stories meant to whip the ladies into an erotic frenzy before they met up with their husbands and lovers .
So, next time you feel the urge to tickle someone's feet, remember that you're part of a long, ticklish tradition that has titillated and amused for centuries!

ORVILLE HUMPERDINCK
IS FAMOUS
FOR BEING THE MAN
WITH FIVE PENISES
THATS RIGHT
HE HAD 5 PENISES!

HOW DID HIS PANTS FIT ?

LIKE A GLOVE

Ok, that was a joke. Orville Humperdinck doesn't exist. however,

The man with two penises, otherwise known as Diphallic Dude, does exist and he has published his second memoir titled:

<u>Double Stuffed: Steamy Tales From My Life With Two Penises.</u>

The name of Diphallic Dudes first memoir is entitled:

**Double Your Pleasure
Double your fun**

**Double Header:
My Life With Two Penises**

**Two Heads
Are Better Than One**

**Daring Adventures
Of The Dynamic Duo**

Two For Tea

Doubles Sandwich

**Richard And Dick
An Unlikely love Story**

Double Header: My Life With Two Penises

The first memoir he wrote,deals with the endeavors he faced growing up with two penises, coming to terms with his bisexuality, and of course, his sex life.

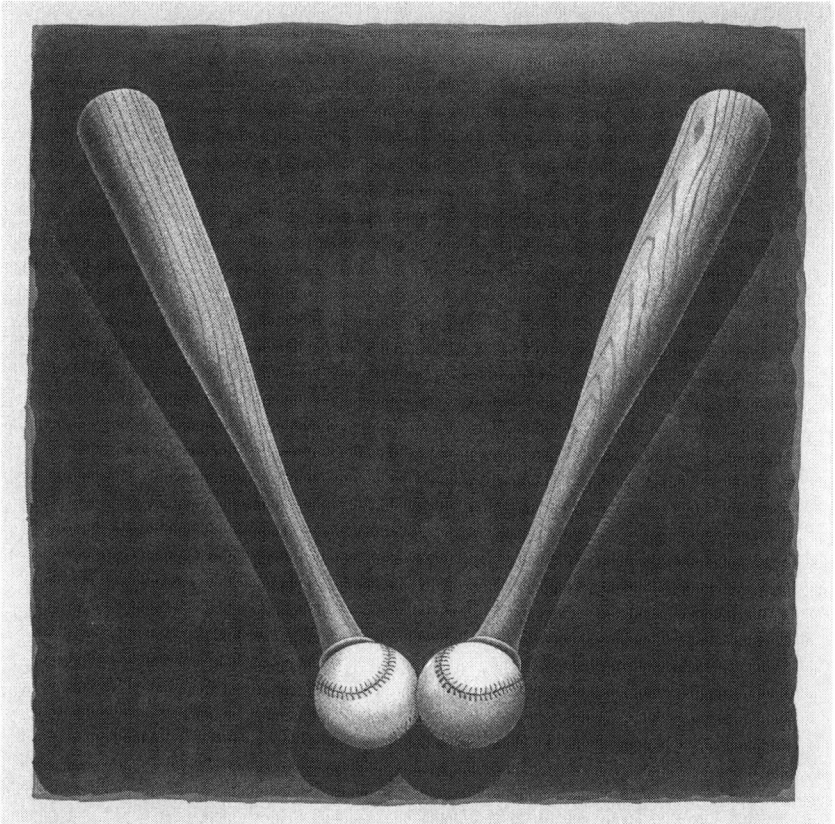

Doubles is a tasty street treat sandwich hailing from Trinidad and Tobago with Indian roots, a breakfast favorite that doubles up as a lunch option or a late-night munchie, especially loved by Trinidadians nursing a hangover.

Diphallia, penile duplication (PD), diphallic terata, or diphallasparatus is an extremely rare developmental abnormality in which a male is born with two penises. Johannes Jacob Wecker was the first documented case in 1609.
How often does it occur?

A.
1 in a million.
B.
1 in 5.5 million.
C.
You have a better chance of winning powerball.

A

1 IN 5.5 MILLION

WHICH STATEMENT IS TRUE

A teaspoon of semen contains 5 calories.

A sperm takes one hour to swim seven inches.

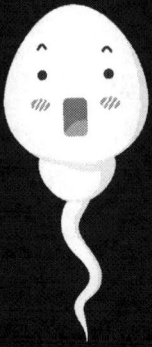

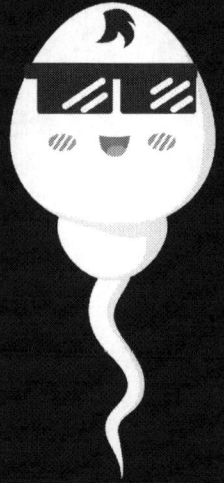

BOTH ARE TRUE

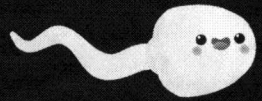

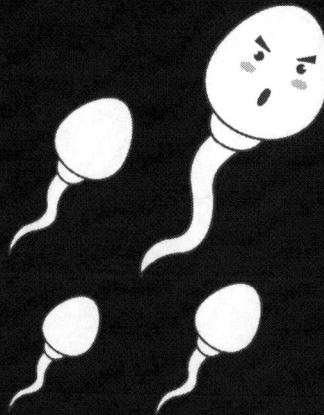
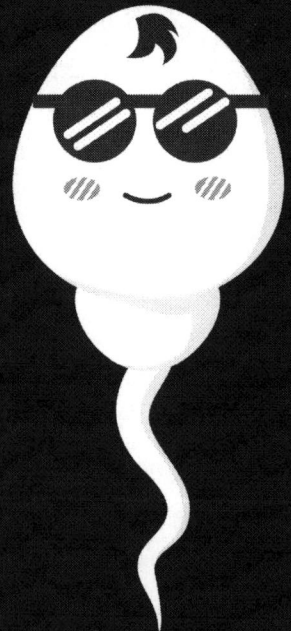

WHY ARE MEN LIKE PANTYHOSE?

THEY EITHER CLING, RUN, OR DON'T FIT IN THE CROTCH.

In the Victorian era, what was considered a cure for male impotence?

A. Cold showers
B. Electric shocks
C. Herbal tea
D. Rooster Semen

B.
Electric
shocks

During the Roman Empire, what did they utilize urine for?

a) Seasoning food
b) Fertilizing crops
c) Whitening clothes
d) Brewing beer

cleaning clothes

what did they use to wash the urine out?

Which ancient civilization believed that the strength of a man's erection was directly related to the size of his nose?

a) Ancient Egypt
b) Ancient Greece
c) Ancient Rome
d) Ancient China
e)The Holy Land

b)
Ancient Greece
because apparently,
the bigger the nose,
the stiffer it grows

WHAT HAPPENED
TO THE JEWISH
NUDIST WHO RAN
INTO THE WAILING
WALL
WITH A RAGING
ERECTION

HE BROKE HIS NOSE.

What creature eats her mate during or after sex ?

Octopus

Black widow

Scorpion

The jumping spider

Roseanne Barr

All the above
Except
Roseanne doesn't swallow.

The black widow spider eats her mate
during or after sex.
The hungry spider can eat as many as
20 lovers—in one day

Peacock jumping spiders are known for their elaborate mating rituals. During the mating season, male peacock spiders perch atop a high surface and wave their hind legs to attract the attention of females. Once a female is spotted, the male produces vibrations to get her attention. The male then performs an intricate dance using a brilliantly colored fan attached to his abdomen. If the female approves, he is allowed to mate. If not, he becomes her next meal

To avoid being eaten, the male octopus typically "jumps on top of the female, they mate in a position where he's as far from her mouth as possible, and when they're done, the male runs away,

Which ancient civilization is known for its elaborate sex manuals and guides?

a)
Aztecs:
Masters of the Mesoamerican Kama Sutra

b)
Vikings:
Pillagers by day, Pleasurers by night

c)
Egyptians:
Hieroglyphic How-To's for the Bedroom

d)
Chinese:
With 6 you get eggroll

d)
Chinese

**A Middle-aged Chinese couple
are laying in bed
and the husband says:
I wanna 69.
His wife says :
Why you want broccoli beef now?**

Who said:

"If God had intended us not to masturbate, He would have made our arms shorter."

A.
Carl Sagan

B.
Confucius

C.
Sigmund Freud

D.
George Carlin

D.
George Carlin

What country has the most sex?

Couples in <u>Greece</u> have the most sex, approximately 164 times per year.
<u>Brazil</u> follows a close second with 145 times per year.
The global average is 103.

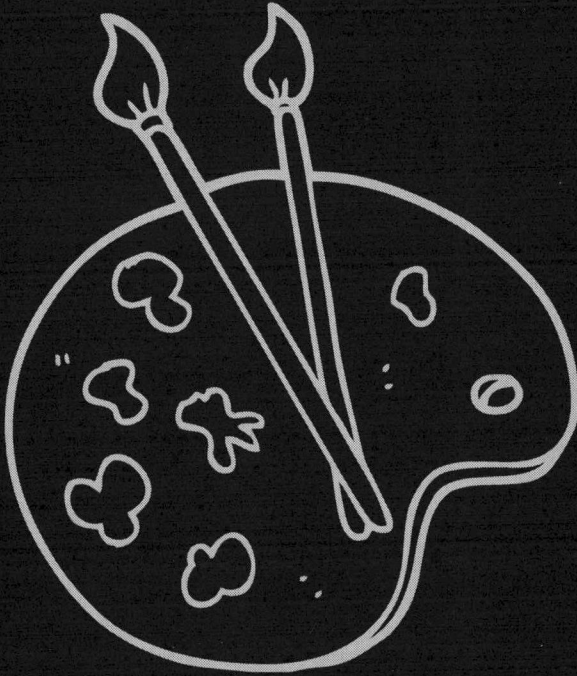

Which famous historical figure was rumored to have kept a collection of over 1,000 erotic artworks?

a) Leonardo da Vinci
b) Vincent van Gogh
c) Pablo Picasso
d) Koko The Gorilla

Pablo Picasso

was found to have a collection of over 1,000 erotic pictures. These artworks were discovered after his death and revealed a different aspect of his artistic expression. Picasso's erotic drawings and paintings are well-known and have contributed to his reputation as an artist who explored various themes and subjects throughout his career.
He was very inspired by Japanese Junga.

Which famous philosopher believed that sexual pleasure was the highest form of happiness?

a) **Aristotle**
b) **Plato**
c) **Socrates**
d) **Confucius**

c) Socrates

"Happiness is unrepented pleasure."

"When desire, having rejected reason and overpowered judgment which leads to right, is set in the direction of the pleasure which beauty can inspire, and when again under the influence of its kindred desires it is moved with violent motion towards the beauty of corporeal forms, it acquires a surname from this very violent motion, and is called love."

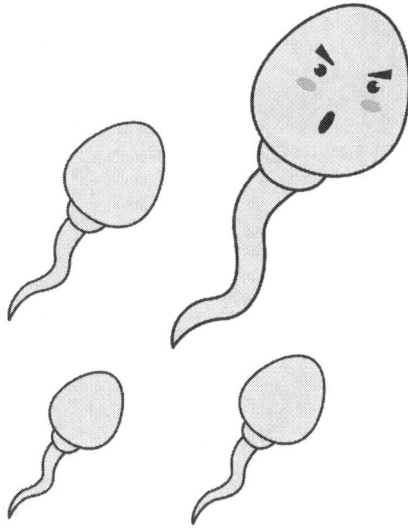

According to the Kinsey Institute, the average speed of sperm during ejaculation is

A) 28 mp

B) Slower than the speed limit in a School Zone

C)Faster than a speeding bullet

D) 5mph

E)Length divided by number of strokes per minute.

28mph

Better wear
a safety helmet!

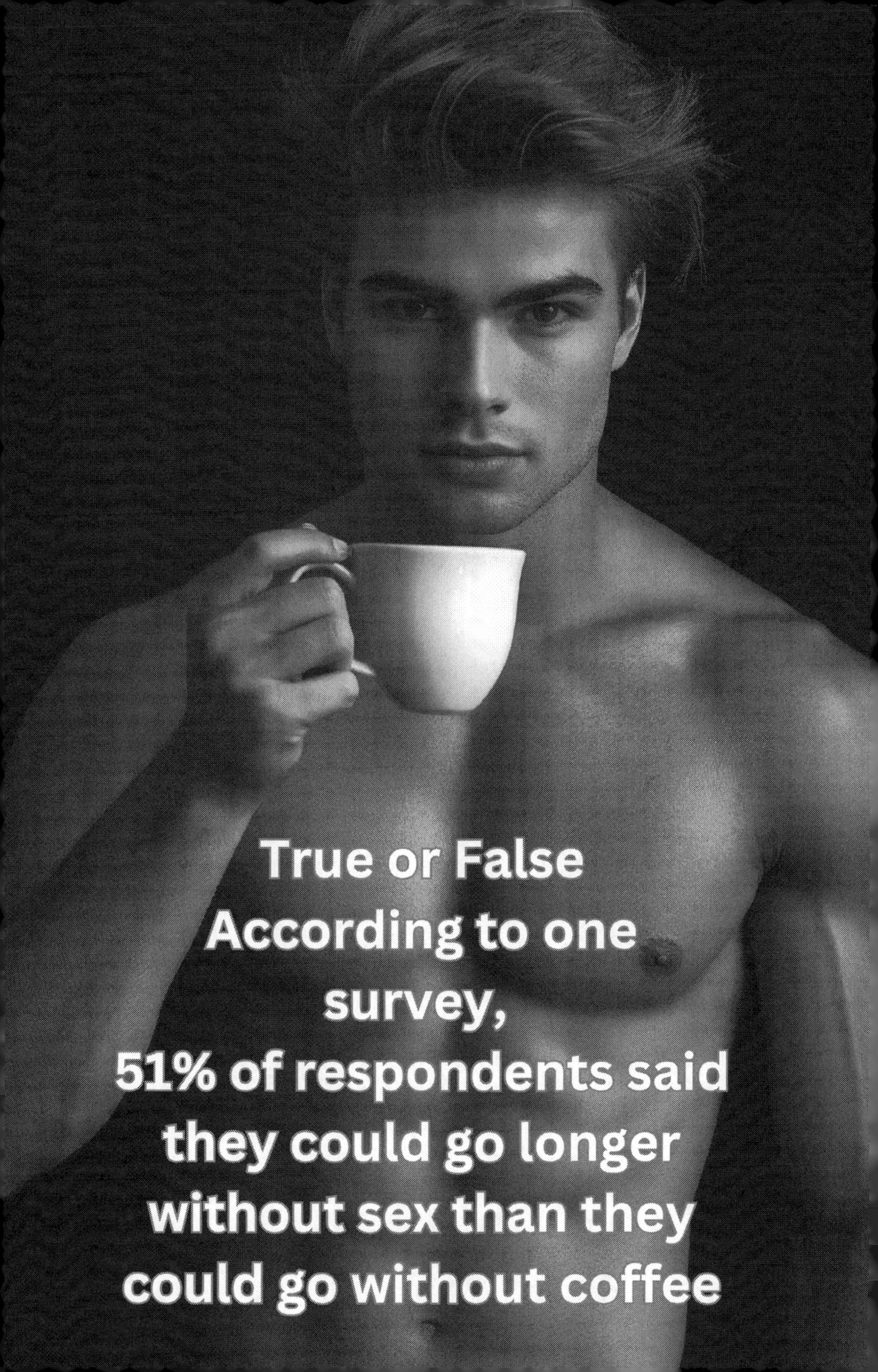

True or False
According to one
survey,
51% of respondents said
they could go longer
without sex than they
could go without coffee

TRUE

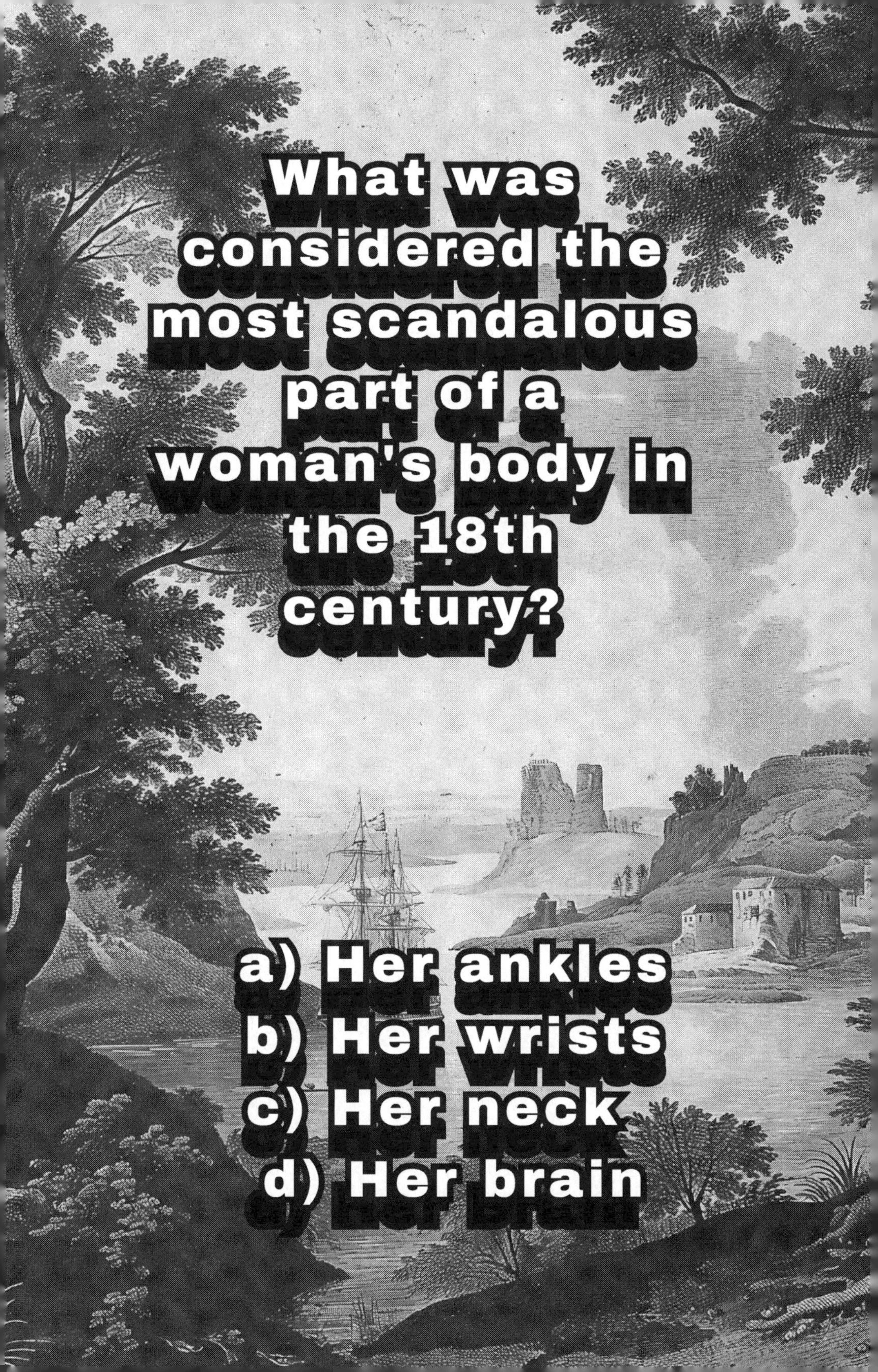

What was considered the most scandalous part of a woman's body in the 18th century?

a) Her ankles
b) Her wrists
c) Her neck
d) Her brain

Ankle

In the 18th century, society was so prudish that the mere sight of a woman's ankles was enough to cause a scandal of epic proportions! Forget about cleavage or curves , Ladies had to keep those ankles under wraps or risk society clutching their pearls in shock. It's ankle-gate, people - the scandalous body part of the century!

In ancient Greece, the term "aphrodisiac" referred to:

A. A delicious Greek dessert
B. A powerful love potion
C. A popular dance move
D. An ancient Greek wrestling move
E. A Black drag queen

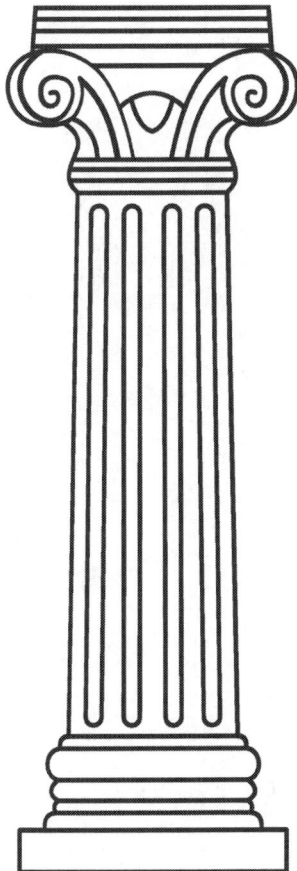

B.

A powerful love potion. Because who needs dessert when you can make sweet love, right?

Which of the following is NOT a mythological aphrodisiac?

A) Eating a love-infused apple from the Garden of Eden.

B) Drinking a vial of mermaid tears.

C) Sprinkling yourself with a crushed powder made from Cupid's arrowheads.

D) Wearing socks with sandals on Mount Olympus.

D)
Wearing socks with sandals on Mount Olympus.

This one is silly

What was the first known contraceptive used in ancient Egypt?

A. Honey
B. Crocodile dung
C. Lemon juice
D. Olive oil

B.
Crocodile dung

Ummmm that tracks

TRUE OR FALSE

THIS JOKE IS FROM FROM 1ST CENTURY A.D.

Emperor Augustus touring his
realm and coming across a man
who bears
a striking resemblance to himself.
Intrigued, he asks the man:
"Was your mother at one time in
service at the palace?"
The man replies:
"No your highness,
but my father was."

TRUE

By the year 1 A.D., Rome transformed from a simple town of local brick and stone into a magnificent city adorned with marble,enhanced water systems, abundant food, luxurious baths, and majestic structures suitable for an emperor. And don't overlook the group of ancient comedians amusing the crowds in the background!

CENTURIES BEFORE THE BORSHCHT BELT BEGAN IN THE EARLY 20TH CENTURY

A 10th Century Anglo-Saxon Joke regarded as the oldest recorded British joke in History

What hangs
at a man's thigh
and wants to poke
the hole that it's
often poked before?'

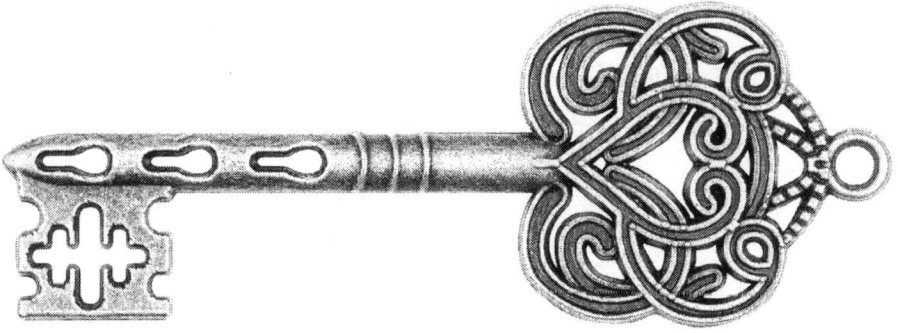

A

KEY

They often hung on a rope or chain tied round the waist.

TRUE OR FALSE

YOU BURN MORE CALORIES MOWING THE LAWN THAN YOU DO HAVING SEX.

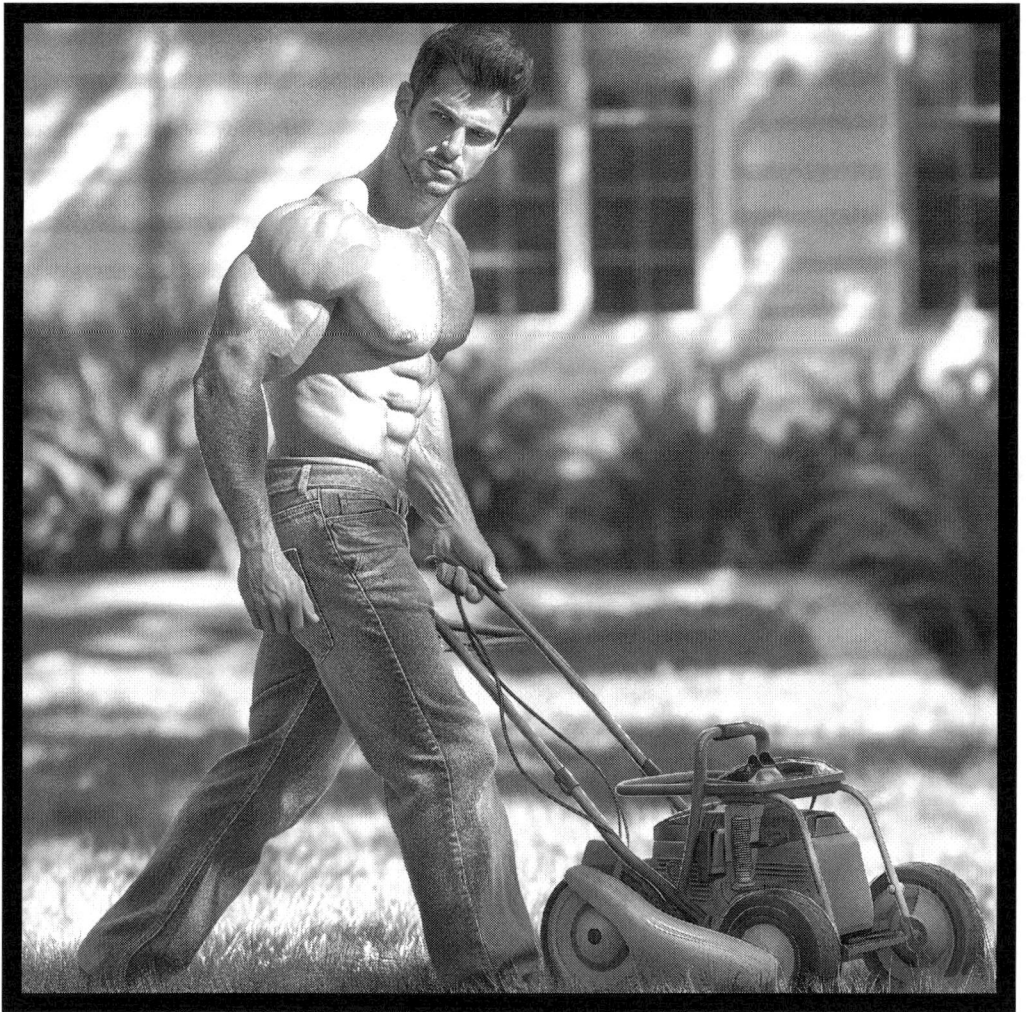

**True
Your looking a
little chunky.
Mow
my lawn honey!**

**In which year
was homosexuality
decriminalized
in the United Kingdom?**
a) 1957
b) 1967
c) 1977
d) 1987

B
1967

What was the 18th century
term for a male prostitute?
a) A gigolo
b) A rake
c) A molly
d) A dandy

"molly" or a "gigolo".
In the 18th century,The term
"molly" was used to describe a
man who engaged in sexual
activities with other men for
money or favors.Gigolos were
typically younger men who
provided entertainment and
romantic attention to wealthy or
older women in exchange for
gifts, money, or favors.

Which of these pickup lines are examples of courtly love from the Middle Ages

A.
You must know many days ago, I was smitten with the arrow of your love, and I tried with all my might to conceal the wound.

B.
Thy cup runneth over, my bone it is dry,
My Dearest one, come,
you're the apple of my eye.

C.
When the divine being made you, he left nothing undone.

D
let's fuck !

B and C
although never
underestimate the
power of D

What was the purpose of the "Codpiece" worn by men during the Renaissance?

a) Protect against the plague... and unwanted advances

 b) Enhance fertility... and advertise availability

 c) Conceal small weapons... love is a battlefield

d) Exaggerate the size of the genitals... and inflate men's egos

e) Accomodate fresh fish oil ... to keep Mr. Happy soft & slippery.

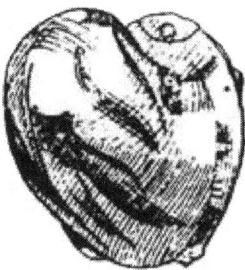

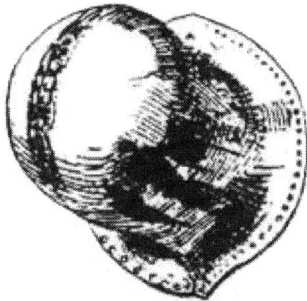

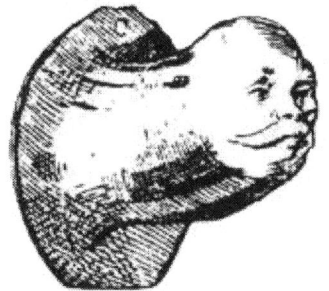

d) To exaggerate
the size of the genitals...
and inflate egos

What terms were used in Victorian England to describe a woman who was sexually promiscuous?

a) Flapper
b) Vixen
c) Harlot
d) Slut
e) Hussy

Harlot!Slut!Hussy!

The term "Flapper" refers to a different cultural phenomenon than the other terms mentioned in the context of Victorian England. The term "Flapper" is associated with the 1920s, particularly in the United States and the United Kingdom, and describes a young woman who was known for her unconventional behavior, including wearing short skirts, bobbing her hair, listening to jazz music, and challenging traditional societal norms. Flappers were often seen as independent, free-spirited, and rebellious against the conservative values of the time. While Flappers were known for their modern and carefree attitudes, the term "Flapper" does not carry the same negative connotations as terms like "harlot," "slut," or "hussy" used in the context of Victorian England.

In the context of Victorian England, the term "vixen" would not typically be used to specifically describe a sexually promiscuous woman. "Vixen" generally refers to a female fox in English, but it can also be used colloquially to describe a woman who is strong-willed, cunning, or feisty. While the term "vixen" might imply a sense of boldness or assertiveness in personality, it does not have the same direct association with sexual promiscuity as terms like "harlot," "slut," or "hussy" did during the Victorian era.

WHAT WOULD BE THE OFFSPRING OF A VIXEN AND A ROOSTER?

A FOXY CHICK.

Who was the primary male fertility god in ancient Egypt?

A) God Min, the "Mr. Fertility" of the divine realm, with his ever-ready phallus.
B) God Bob, the deity with a knack for making lettuce grow and love blossom.
C) God Stan, the feathered headdress enthusiast who had a special fondness for phallic figurines.

A)
God Min,
the "Mr. Fertility" of the divine realm,
with his ever-ready phallus.

Which famous poet kept labled envelopes with clippings of his many lovers pubic hair?

A. William Shakespeare

B. T.S. Elliot

C. Lord Byron

D. Percy Byshe Shelley

E. Dr. Seuss

LORD BYRON (George Gordon)
After a love affair, of which he had many, Byron would take his partner's pubic hair and store it in an envelope that he would label with their name.

Can you imagine if it was Dr. Seuss?

Would you? Could you? Clip your curly hair.
from somewhere up here... to way down there?

Would you? Could you?
Eat me
on my back,
where its big and bushy
till it meets my tushy crack?

I love the stench

where the curly hairs grow.

Can I wear your pussy

like a french chapeau?

WHO IS RUMORED TO HAVE CREATED THE FIRST ANCIENT VIBRATOR?

CLEOPATRA

talk about bee-stung lips

RUMOR HAS IT
SHE SEALED, ANGRY BEES,
INSIDE OF AN EMPTY GOURD

The Erotic Papyrus Of Turin

A.
Contains graphic pictures of Egyptian pornography

B.
Contains hieroglyphic dirty talk

C.
Romantic letters written by Jesus

D.
An ancient treatise on sex 1000 years older than the Kama Sutra

E.
Contains humorous satire

All but C

The Turin Papyrus is 3000 years old from the era of Ramesses III, roughly a millennium before the Kama Sutra hit the shelves! Among the ancient illustrations, there are cheeky comments hinting at joy and pleasure. Scribbled above one image is a poetic note:

"Come behind me with your love, Oh! Sun, you have found out my heart, it is agreeable work."

True or False
Men
who help
with housework
tend to have
less sex

False
<u>Men</u> who help with housework tend to have MORE sex

Who said "Sex is like bridge if you don't have a good partner, you better have a good hand"

A) Clark cable
B) Stu Ungar
C) George Burns
D) Woody Allen

Woody Allen

♠

Stu Ungar,
known as "The Kid" for his youthful
looks, was a legendary card player.
Stu won his first gin tournament at
just 10 years old, paving the way for
his poker stardom in the late 1970s.

How did Queen Elizabeth I of England maintain her virginity?

a) By wearing a chastity belt made of solid gold

b) By constantly eating raw garlic and pickles

c) By surrounding herself with a horde of loyal pet corgis

d) By declaring herself married to the kingdom of England

d)

Declaring herself married to the kingdom of England

Queen Elizabeth I of England, famously dubbed the "Virgin Queen,"never married or had children,Some history buffs think she was head over heels for her queenly duties, seeing marriage as a threat to her power. Others reckon her folks' rocky love story left her scarred, making her dodge the marriage bullet just in case.

By the way, calling her the "Virgin Queen" wasn't a purity certificate. It was more of a fancy label highlighting her solo status and the lack of royal heirs running around.

How did people in the 16th century determine the gender of an unborn child?

a) By analyzing the shape of the mother's belly button

b) By consulting a fortune-telling chicken

c) By observing the position of the baby in the womb during a lunar eclipse

d) By tossing a boiled egg and a potato in the air and seeing which one landed first

d)
**By tossing a boiled egg
and a potato in the air
and seeing which
one landed first**

According to this belief, if an
egg is caught, it indicates that
the baby will be a girl, while if
a potato is caught, it signifies
that the baby will be a boy.

TRUE OR FALSE? CHARLIE CHAPLIN LIKED CREAM PIE SEX

True

According to film historian Kevin Brownwing, author of "The Golden Grope: A History of Hollywood Harassment", Charlie Chaplin made use of the 'casting couch communicating with the actresses he was 'auditioning' via caption cards and mime, supposedly to test their ability to 'perform' in silent movies,"
"The cards would become ever more lewd and suggestive as he got them to undress, and he would fondle their breasts in an exaggerated silent movie-acting manner, silently conveying his growing sexual arousal through grotesque facial mugging and crudely mimed gestures. Eventually, he would get them to stand, naked, at one end of the audition room and throw custard pies at them. Finally, he would lick the girls clean with his tongue before making love to them on an actual casting couch, whilst a pianist played appropriate background music."

Which of the following was NOT a popular term for a condom in the 16th century?

a) Love sock
b) French letter
c) Scabbard of love
d) Sausage skin

c)
Scabbard of love

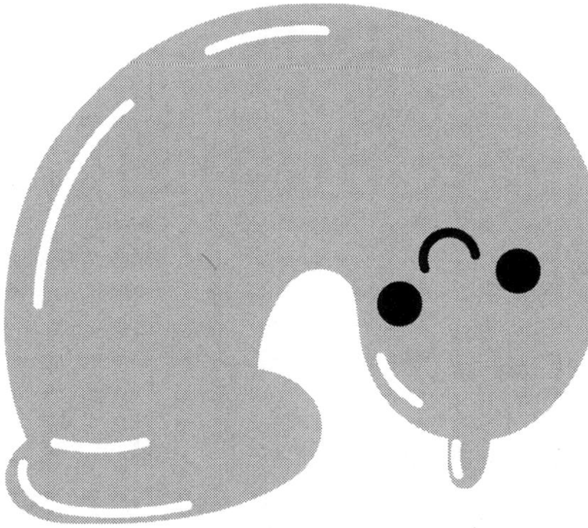

"French letter" is indeed a historical term that was used to refer to a condom. The term originated in the 18th century and remained in use throughout the 19th and 20th centuries. The term "French letter" was commonly used in English-speaking countries as a euphemism for a condom, likely because French manufacturers were known for producing condoms during that time.

Who holds the record for The loudest Penis?

Micronecta Scholtzi,
a tiny insect with big ambitions. This minuscule critter, measuring just two millimeters, has a secret weapon to woo the women. He rubs his micropenis against its abdomen, creating a chirping noise that can reach an ear-popping 99.2 decibels. That's as ear piercing as the front row at an an Ozzie Osborn concert!

This tiny Casanova engages in a technique called stridulation. By serenading potential mates with its unique musical talents, the Micronecta Scholtzi aims to attract a partner for some insect romance. Move over, smooth-talking humans, this little insect knows how to make some noise!

**Who invented
the first electric vibrator?**

a) Thomas Edison
b) Benjamin Franklin
c) Nikola Tesla
d) Alexander Graham Bell
E) Dr. Joseph Mortimer Granville

E)
Dr. Joseph Mortimer Granville

The first electromechanical vibrator was actually invented by British physician Dr. Joseph Mortimer Granville in the late 19th century. Granville's invention, known as the "electro-mechanical vibrator," was originally designed as a medical device to relieve muscle pain and fatigue. However, it soon became popular for treating "female hysteria," a common diagnosis at the time for a range of symptoms that included anxiety, irritability, and sexual frustration.

The Kama Sutra is an extensive guide on intimate relationships with:

A)
ten types of kisses.
B)
sixty-four different caresses.
C)
eight variations on oral sex.
D)
eighty-four positions for intercourse.
E)
All the above

E)
All the above
ten types of kisses, sixty-four
different caresses, eight variations
on oral sex, and eighty-four
positions for intercourse.
Interestingly, the author, Mallanga
Vatsyayana, was believed to be
celibate and wrote the book
through divine knowledge.

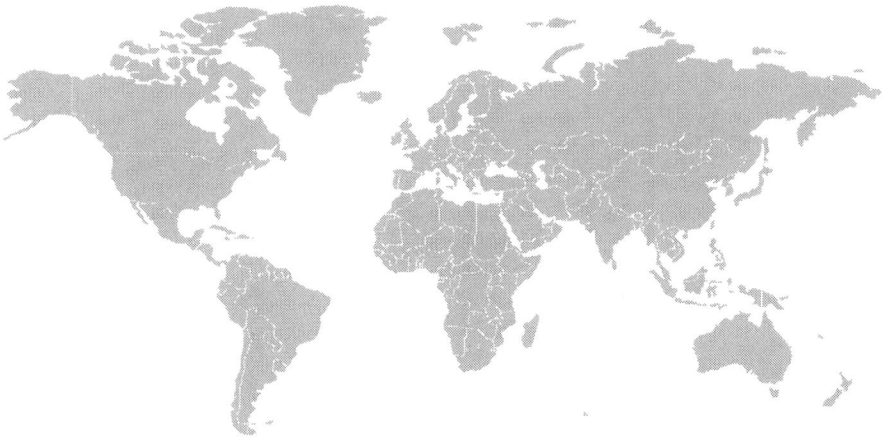

Which country has the highest average number of sexual partners per person?

a) United States
b) France
c) Sweden
d) Australia

b)
France

When referring to
their sexual exploits
Which historical
figure famously said,

"I may not have been
the first, but I
certainly made it
popular"

a) Casanova
b) Cleopatra
c) Marilyn Monroe
d) Henry VIII

Casanova

the ultimate charmer known for his romantic escapades and tell-all memoirs.Casanova's love tales unfolded during the years 1725 to 1798, as he gallivanted across Europe, wooing women from all walks of life. His book, "The Story of My Life," spills all the steamy details. But hey, let's remember, tracking down the exact origin of this quote might be as tricky as catching a sly Casanova in the act!

True or False:
In ancient Greece,
the word "orgasm"
was used to describe
a type of festive gathering.

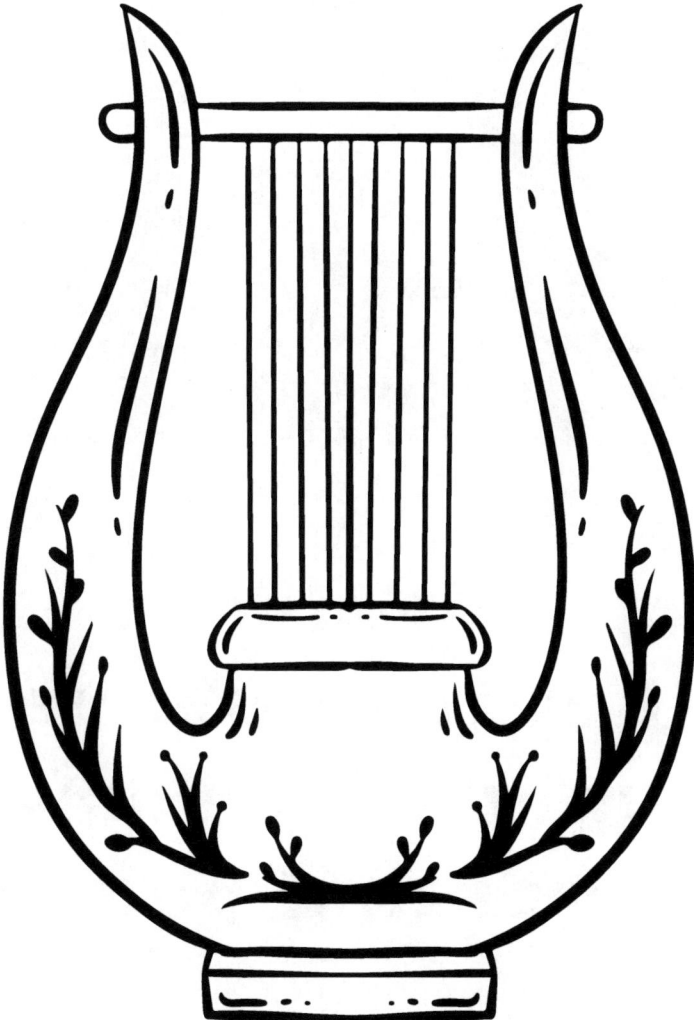

**False
(but it would have
made for some
interesting parties!)**

Which famous painter was known for including subtle sexual symbolism in their artworks?

a) Michelangelo
b) Salvador Dalí
c) Leonardo da Vinci
d) Koko the gorilla

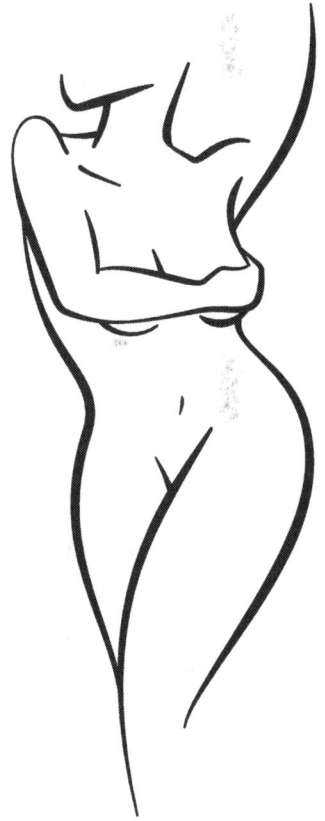

b) Salvador Dalí

Salvador Dalí was a surrealist artist known for incorporating dreamlike imagery and symbolism, including subtle and sometimes overt sexual themes, in his paintings. His works often featured peculiar and provocative imagery that invited viewers to explore the depths of the subconscious mind.

Which famous artist painted with poop?

A. Vincent Van Gogh

B. Pablo Picasso

C. Koko the Gorilla

D. Kieth Haring

Pablo Picasso painted using his daughter's poop. Pablo Picasso painted an apple in his work "Still Life" (1938) with his daughter Maya's poop. His granddaughter,says he loved the pigment, saw it as "smooth as oil".

You totally thought it was me didnt you?

Why was the god Min associated with lettuce in ancient Egypt?

A) Because lettuce was believed to have the power of turning people into rabbits for a day.

B) Because Egyptian lettuce had a milk-like sap that resembled semen, making it a fitting symbol for fertility.

C) Because the ancient Egyptians loved tossing the salad, and Min had a special affinity for leafy greens.

B)

Because Egyptian lettuce had a milk-like sap that resembled semen, making it a fitting symbol for fertility.

**Lettuce have sex!
Not to be confused with
head of lettuce.
Not to be confused with
Hedda Lettuce the drag queen!**

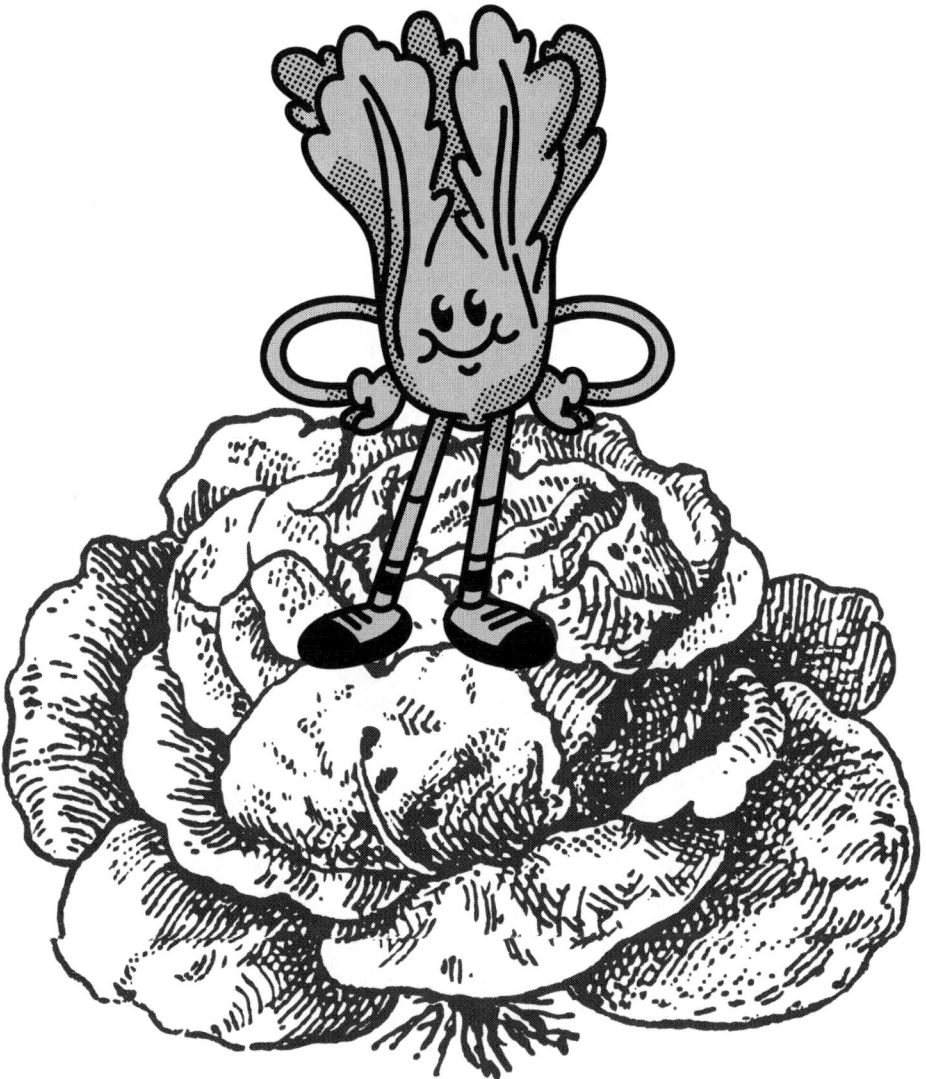

Which famous composer
Wrote a song entitled
"Lick me in the ass"

A. Ludvig Von Beethoven
B.Johannes Brahms
C.Wolfgang Amadeus Mozart
D.Paul Simon
E.Boy George

**Wolfgang Amadeus Mozart
was said to be a fan of
analingus.The 18th century
composer wrote over 600 pieces
of symphony music,**
including
"Leck mich im Arsch"
**which translates to
"Lick me in the ass,"**
The Lyrics include :
"Lick me in the ass, quickly, quickly!"

Which animal species is known for engaging in "sexual role reversal," where males take on traditionally female reproductive roles?

a) Penguins
b) Seahorses
c) Gorillas
d) Elephants

b)
Seahorses
(talk about breaking
gender norms!)

True or False:
The term "drag queen"
originated from the phrase
"dressed as a girl"
in Shakespearean theatre.

The phrase "drag" may have its roots in Shakespearean Theater, where actors often donned different gender roles due to the all-male casts. However, the term "drag queen" didn't make its grand entrance until the 20th century within the vibrant underground LGBT+ scene in the US. From there, it blossomed into its own, symbolizing male performers who dazzle audiences in over-the-top femininity. While gender-bending acts have a rich history in the spotlight, the term "drag queen" and its fabulous essence took the stage much later.

Which LGBTQ+ rights activist famously said, "Why be a sheep when you can be a fabulous unicorn"?

a) Harvey Milk
b) Marsha P. Johnson
c) Ellen DeGeneres
d) RuPaul

d)
RuPaul
(always inspiring us to embrace our true selves!)

Who said:
"Eating an ice cream cone 'provocatively' in public can send out a message, if you dare."

A. Marilyn Monroe
B. liberace
C. Dr. Phil
D. Dr. Ruth
E. Linda Lovelace

D)
Dr. Ruth

Which ancient civilization believed that having sex before battle would bring them good luck?

a) Egyptian
b) Greek
c) Roman
d) Aztec

b)
Greeks were encouraged to have sex with their fellow soldiers.

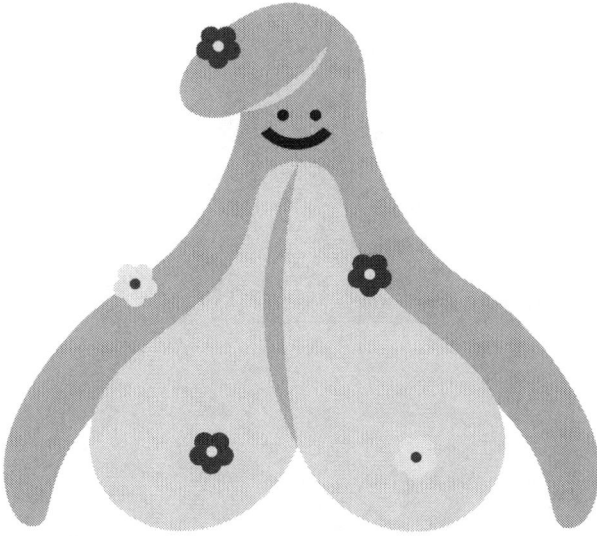

In the Middle Ages, what was the common belief about the clitoris?

a) It was considered a symbol of purity and divine pleasure

b) It was believed to be non-existent in women.

c) It was associated with witchcraft and evil.

d) It was considered a sign of fertility and good luck.

Witchcraft
and
evil

Who coined the term
"sexual revolution"
to describe the cultural changes
surrounding sexuality in the 1960s?
a) Sigmund Freud
b) Alfred Kinsey
c) Hugh Hefner
d) Mick Jagger

The British are coming
The women are coming
The men are coming
Everyone is coming

Kinsey

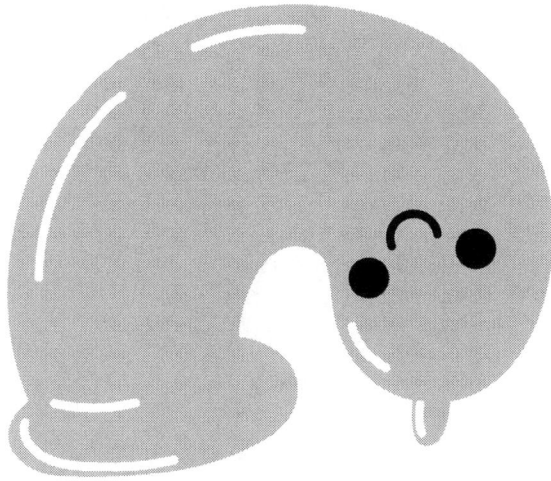

Who was known for their
unconventional approach
to sex education?

a) Sigmund Freud
b) Marie Curie
c) Dr. Ruth Westheimer
d) Leonardo da Vinci

c)

Dr. Ruth Westheimer

4 feet 7 inches (1.39 m) tall

A German-American sex therapist, talk show host, author, professor, and Holocaust survivor.She served as a sniper in the Israeli Army.

"Though I am only 4 feet 7 inches tall, with a gun in my hand I am the equal of a soldier who's 6 feet 7—and perhaps even at a slight advantage, as I make a smaller target."

Who said
"Love
ain't nothing but sex
misspelled..."

A. Harry Truman
B. Harlan Ellison
C. Lauren Bacall
D. Justin Beaver

Harlan Ellison,
the mastermind behind mind-
bending tales in science fiction,
fantasy, and speculative fiction.
With his daring flair, he
fearlessly explored hot topics
and snagged prestigious awards
like the Hugo and Nebula.

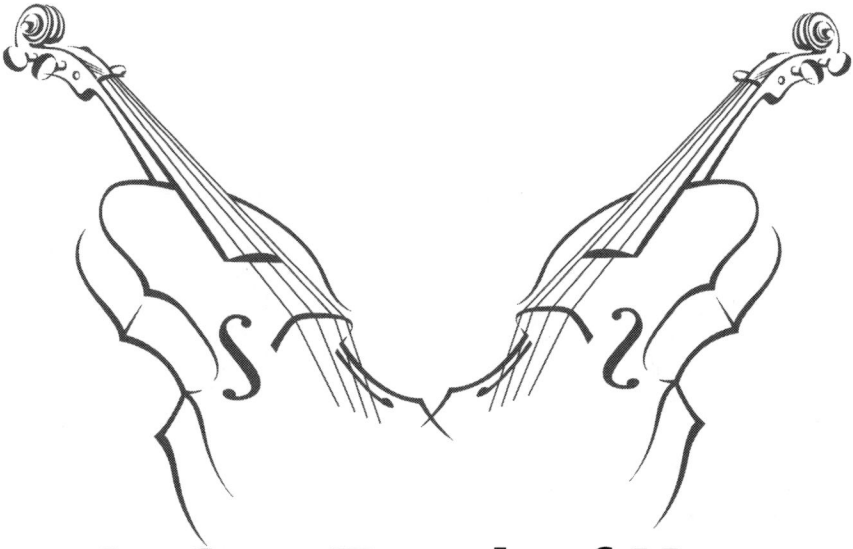

In One Touch of Venus, Ogden Nash and S. J. Perelman said :

"Love is not the dying moan of a distant violin- It's—-"

A) the roar of a lion
B)The squeal of a pig
C)the triumphant twang of a bedspring.

c)

Love is not the dying moan of a distant
violin-
It's—-

the triumphant
twang of a bedspring.

Who said:

"Where there's marriage without love there will be love without marriage."

A.Fred Flintstone

B.Casanova

C.Benjamin Franklin

D.Dean Martin

Benjamin Franklin

Who was at the center of the diamond necklace affair ?

a) Marie Antoinette
b) Marie Curie
c) Marie Kondo
d) Marie Claire

Marie Antoinette
A pearl necklace is something else altogether

Love in a Tub or a Cure for a Cold.

Which sexually transmitted infection was prevalent in the 18th century?

a) Syphilis
b) HIV/AIDS
c) Gonorrhea
d) Chlamydia

a)

Syphilis

It spread like gossip
at a tea party,
leaving its mark on history
like a regrettable tattoo.

What was the primary purpose of chastity belts in the 18th century?

a) Preventing adultery and extramarital affairs

b) Enhancing sexual pleasure for both partners

c) Maintaining modesty and virtue in women

d) Providing protection against sexually transmitted infections

— Pas de veine, mon pauvre petit, cette fois il m'a mis un cadenas à lettres !...

c) Maintaining modesty and virtue in women

Because nothing says "romance" like a metal accessory that screams "hands off" louder than a peacock in a library.

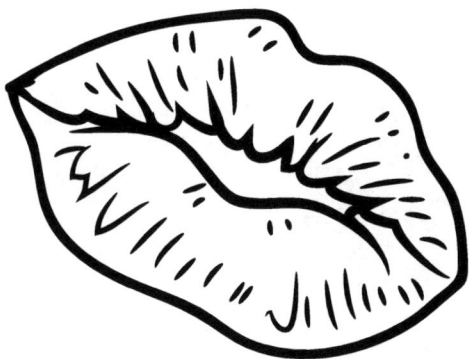

Who said :

*"Whoever named it necking
was a poor judge of anatomy."*

A Groucho Marx
B Marilyn Monroe
C My Gynecoligist
D Dr. Ruth
E Cary Grant

GROUCHO MARX

How many minutes does the average person spend kissing during their lifetime?

a) 20,160 minutes
b) 10,080 minutes
c) 40,320 minutes
d) Too many to count, it's a lifetime supply of smooches!

The average person spends
20,160 minutes kissing during a lifetime, which is 336 hours, 14 days, or 2 weeks. A fortnight. The same time as 3 eruptions on Jupiter IO.

How would you describe the men depicted in the "Turin Erotic Papyrus"?

A) Ancient Egyptian heartthrobs, with perfectly coiffed hair and chiseled physiques.
B) Balding, unshaven, and slightly disheveled, like the 70's porn stars of yore.
C) Mysterious and enigmatic, with a rugged charm that still makes hearts flutter today.

B)

Balding, unshaven, and slightly disheveled, like the 70's porn stars of yore.

How many calories does the average person burn during 30 minutes of active sex?

a) Approximately 200 calories
b) Enough to justify an extra slice of pizza
c) A whopping 450 calories if they screw like a champ!
d) Who cares about calories when you're having so much fun?

a.

During 30 minutes of active sex, the average person burns approximately 200 calories.

The same as 1.45 oz of a Snickers Chocolate Bar

A full bar is 2.oz

The Egyptians believed that sex was a sacred act of creation. According to their mythology, the first god Atum created the world through:

A) Kissing a magical frog.
B) Castrating himself.
C) Copulating with a snake while eating an apple.
D) Masturbation.

D

The ancient Egyptians took the idea of "act of creation" quite literally! According to their mythology, the first god, Atum, didn't need a partner to create the world. Nope, he took matters into his own hands, literally! Yes, you heard it right – Atum single-handedly brought the world into existence through the power of...erm...masturbation! The Egyptians believed that the first gods were actually twins, and they came into being through a mighty ejaculation. Talk about a divine splash! And if you thought that was wild, guess what they considered the earliest evidence of life? Semen! They saw it as the ultimate proof that life was, well, in the making.

So, next time you think about ancient Egypt, remember that their views on creation were definitely a bit more hands-on than you might have imagined!

What was the ancient Sumerians' stance on masturbation?

A) They thought it was a way to summon aliens.

B) They believed it enhanced sexual prowess, like a secret superpower.

C) They considered it a form of entertainment for the gods.

D) A sin punishable by flogging

Sumerian warrior with bulls

B)

They believed it enhanced sexual prowess, like a secret superpower.

What can be said about the women depicted in the "Turin Erotic Papyrus"?

A) They are portrayed as strong and independent, breaking societal norms of the time.

B) They are the embodiment of beauty in ancient Egypt, setting the standard for attractiveness.

C) They are depicted with a humorous twist, showcasing exaggerated features and comical situations.

B)
They are the embodiment of beauty in ancient Egypt, setting the standard for attractiveness. The men were balding, unshaven, and slightly disheveled.

Who turned part of the imperial palace into a whorehouse, in which the wives of leading senators and dignitaries were made to serve as prostitutes.

A. Rasputin
B. Donald Trump
C. Mitch McConnell
D. Caligula
E. Qianlong

Caligula

Gaius Caesar Augustus Germanicus, rocked the Roman Empire as emperor from AD 37 until his unfortunate exit in AD 41.

Caligula was known for his wild antics, enjoying gladiator fights, horse races, and theater shows. He even participated in gladiator training and had the Senate's approval to manipulate gladiator numbers in Rome. At the tender age of four or five, Gaius joined his father, mother, and siblings on the campaign in Germania. Although he was named after Gaius Julius Caesar, his father's troops lovingly dubbed him "Caligula" ('little boot').

What did ancient Egyptian men suffering from impotence do to seek divine assistance?

A) They hired personal cheerleaders to chant encouraging phrases.
B) They made offerings of phallic figurines to the god Min, hoping for a magical boost.
C) They consumed massive amounts of lettuce , harnessing the power of green leafy vegetables.

B)
They would make offerings of phallic figurines to the god Min, hoping for a magical boost.

What was the item that went on display in 1927 at New York City's Museum of French Art?

A. Napoleon's hat
B. Napoleon's sword
C. Napoleon's penis
D. Josephine's IUD

Napoleon's Penis

How was Napoleon's penis described in 1927 at New York City's Museum of French Art?

A. Hung like a jury
   with a nagging doubt.

B. He's a grower not a shower.

C. A shriveled sea horse.

D. One inch long like a grape.

C and D

I heard it resembled
"a shriveled sea horse,
a maltreated strip
of buckskin shoelace,
a shriveled eel,
a small baby's finger,
one inch long,
like a grape."

Which historical figure got so turned on by a cow's genitals, he had copies made of gold, and sent them around the empire, with orders to find a woman similarly endowed.

A. Peter The Great

B. Ottoman Sultan Ibrahim I

C. King Edward VII

D. Caligula

E. Nero

B.
Ottoman Sultan Ibrahim I

A 350-pound woman with matching parts was eventually found, and she became one of his favorite concubines

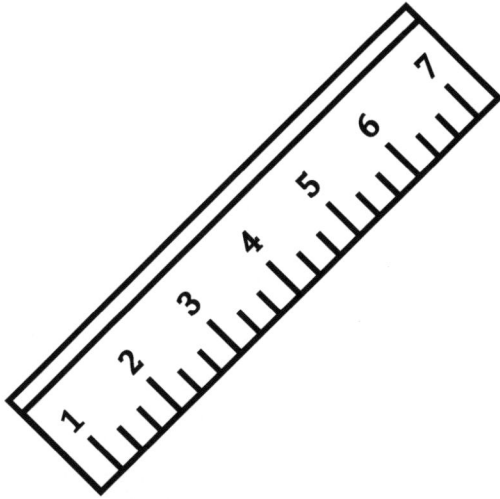

Who said:

"When it comes to sex, the most important six inches are the ones between the ears."

A) Marilyn Monroe

B) Oprah

C) Dr. Ruth

D) Napoleon

E) Benjamin Franklin

Dr. Ruth

What was the name of the men's club in London where Benjamin Franklin enjoyed his "wenching" adventures?

A) The Devils Den
B) The Rendezvous
C) The Hellfire Club
D) The Fox and Hound
E) Bangers and Mash

The Hellfire Club

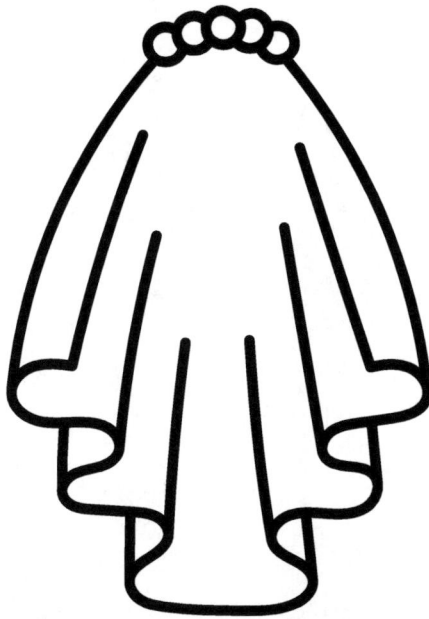

Who was it that "castrated the boy Sporus and actually tried to make a woman of him; -married him with all the usual ceremonies, including a dowry and a bridal veil, took him to his house attended by a great throng, and treated him as his wife."

A. Caligula
B.Tiberious
C.Truman Capote
D.linsdsey Graham
E.Nero
F. Socrates

E.

NERO

Who was so fat and out of shape, he had an extraordinary and highly imaginative chair named "siege d'amourto" specifically designed to position his partners just right for access,allowing him have sex without crushing them.

A. Heliogabulous
B.King herod
C.King Edward VII
D.Chris Farley

King Edward VII
It's good to be the king!

Who held a beggar hostage, flogging and pouring hot wax on her, and was arrested for knocking out prostitutes with roofies and sodomizing them?

A.Patrick Bateman

B.Jeffrey Epstein

C.Donald Trump Jr.

D.Marquis De Sade

E.Bill Cosby

MARQUIS DE SADE

**Donatien Alphonse François
(2 June 1740 – 2 December 1814)
French writer, libertine, political
activist and nobleman best known for
his libertine novels and imprisonment
for sex crimes, blasphemy and
pornography.**

WHO, ALTHOUGH CELIBATE, HAD A HABIT OF COMPULSIVE MASTURBATION?

A. Charles M. Shulz

B. Hans Christian Anderson

C. Mother Theresa

D. Edgar Allan poe

**HANS CHRISTIAN
ANDERSON**

Who said:
"You don't quit when your tired- you quit when the gorilla is tired!"

A. Robert Strauss

B. Ronald Reagan

C. Koko the Gorilla

D. Jane Goodall

Robert Strauss

The American actor, graced the
silver screen in the golden era of
Hollywood during the 1950s.
His standout performance in
"Stalag 17"
landed him an
Academy Award nomination
for Best Supporting Actor.

If you said Koko your racist

How did the founding fathers identify George Washington's hookers?

Splinters in their nipples!

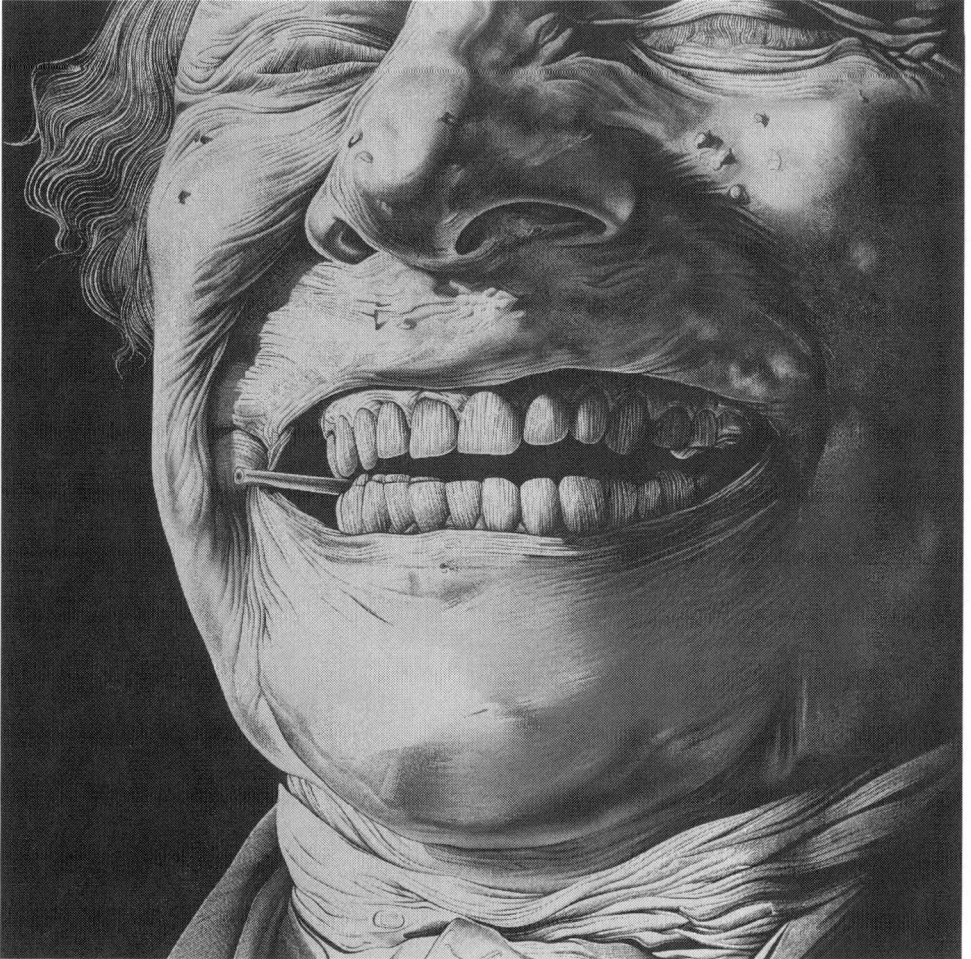

Contrary to popular belief, George Washington's dentures were not made of wood. They were crafted from materials like human and animal teeth, ivory, lead-tin alloy, and silver alloy.

Which historical figure preserved his wife's corpse in honey and and kept "fulfilling his animalistic desires" with the cadaver for seven years after her death?

A.Ghengis Kahn

B.Zhengde Emperor

C.Crown Prince Sado

D.king Herod

Herod the Great

(74 BC – circa 1 AD)

is the king from the New Testament who ordered the Massacre of the Innocents when Jesus was born. Herod is resonsible for building the Second Temple in Jerusalem, and the fortress of Masada.

Herod didn't just stroll into power; he took the throne by tying the knot with Mariamne, a royal gem from Judea's Hasmonean Dynasty. The catch? Herod had murdered many of her relatives.Herod was head over heels with her great beauty. Things took a wild turn when Herod uncovered Mariamne plotting against him with their sons and had her and their offspring executed. Plunged into a deep depression he was unable to let her go. Literally. According to the Talmud, Herod had Mariamne's corpse preserved in honey, and kept "fulfilling his animalistic desires" with the cadaver for the next seven years.

**Who had sex
with his dead wife's
lookalike half sister
when she was 14?**

A. Heliogabulous
B.Maximilien Robespierre
C.King Herod
D.Thomas Jefferson

> "All men are created equal, that they are endowed by their Creator with certain inalienable Rights, that among these are Life, Liberty and the pursuit of Happiness"

D.

Thomas Jefferson

Sally Hemmings (1773 – 1835) had quite the family tree twist - she was the half-sister of Jefferson's wife, Martha Wayles Jefferson, thanks to Martha's father and one of his slaves. With a striking resemblance to her older half-sister, Sally caught the eye of Thomas Jefferson after Martha's passing in 1782. At age 13 or 14 –Jefferson turned his dead wife's lookalike half-sister into his concubine.

What U.S. President called his penis Jumbo?

Lyndon B. Johnson
called his Johnson
Jumbo
After using the urinal he would"sometimes swing around still holding his member and exclaim, "Have you ever seen anything as big as this?"

Who admitted in his autobiography <u>Confessions</u> that he was a complete submissive: "To be at the knees of an imperious mistress, to obey her orders, to have to beg her pardon, have been for me the sweetest delights."

A. Jean-Jacques Rousseau
B. Voltaire
C. Mitch Mcconnell
D. Benjamin Franklin

Philosopher
Jean-Jacques Rousseau

Even as a child
he liked to be spanked.
A LOT!

*"Freedom
is the power to choose our own chains"*

Which of the Founding Fathers had so many affairs with women it caused him to lose a leg?

A. Benjamin Franklin

B.Gouverneur Morris

C.Benjamin Rush

D.Thomas Paine

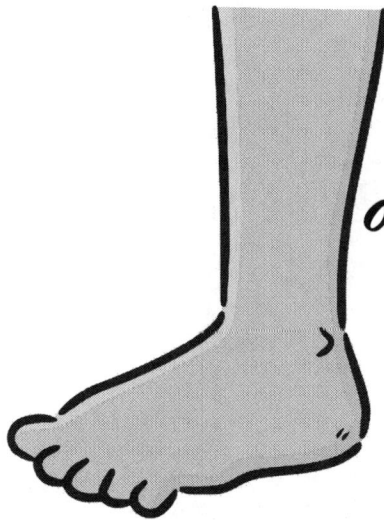

give me
pussy
or give me...

Gouverneur Morris

One of the less recognized Founding Fathers, Gouverneur Morris, has been widely portrayed as a libertine in terms of his romantic pursuits. Despite having only one leg, Morris engaged in numerous affairs with women. Legend has it that he lost his leg when he was caught by a lover's husband. Trying to flee, Morris was allegedly run over by a carriage, resulting in the loss of his leg.

Which of the Founding Fathers' was completely convinced that masturbation, or "self-abuse," caused tuberculosis, memory loss, and epilepsy.

A. John Hancock
B. John Adams
C. John William Jacob Heimer Smith
D. Benjamin Rush
E. Thomas Jefferson
D. All the above

Benjamin Rush

Back in the days of powdered wigs and quills, medicine was a weird and wacky world. Benjamin Rush, a Founding Father who signed the Declaration of Independence,was convinced that self abuse could actually trigger tuberculosis, memory lapses, and even epilepsy!

Thank goodness
they didn't have strobe lights yet !

Which U.S. President referred to his penis as "Jerry"

A. JFK

B. William Howard Taft

C. George W. bush

D. Warren G. Harding

Warren G. Harding

The 29th president of the United States had a secret pen-pal situation with his sweetheart Carrie Fulton Phillips. It was all hush-hush for almost ten years until 2014 when their coded love notes were unveiled. Turns out, Harding had a special nickname for his penis "Jerry".

Oh, the scandal!

He wrote:

"Jerry - you recall Jerry... came in while I was pondering your notes in glad reflection, and we talked about it. He was strongly interested, and elated and clung to discussion. He told me to say that you are the best and darlingest in the world, and if he could have but one wish, it would be to be held in your darling embrace and be thrilled by your pink lips that convey the surpassing rapture of human touch and the unspeakable joy of love's surpassing embrace. I cordially agree with all he said. Perhaps it is not important maybe it is not even interesting, but he is devotedly, exclusively, for you."

Which U.S. President
fathered the most children?

A. Thomas Jefferson

B.John Adams

C.John Tyler

D. William Henry Harrison

John Tyler takes the crown for being the daddiest daddy among all US presidents! This history-making president, number 10 on the list, had a whopping 15 little ones running around. He had eight kids with his first wife, Letitia Christian, and another seven with his second wife, Julia Gardner.Plus possibly "some" out of wedlock.

Thomas jefferson 14 plus
William Henry Harrison 11 plus

Which of the founding fathers loved older women, having written: "In all your amours, you should prefer old women to young ones," because they make better lovers and "the sin is less." He also says "there is no hazard of children" and they will prevent you from "ruining health and fortune among mercenary prostitutes."

A. John Hancock

B. James Madison

C. Benjamin Franklin

D. Joe Biden

C

Benjamin Franklin's

"Advice to a Young Man on the Choice of a Mistress" was a secretly-circulated letter to a young man in 1745 (published 1961)

"regarding what is below the Girdle, it is impossible...
to tell an old one from
a young one."

"Lastly, they are so grateful!"

WHY WAS
MARIE ANTOINETTE

DISSAPOINTED
ON HER
WEDDING NIGHT?

SHE THOUGHT ALL RULERS WERE 12 INCHES

Who said:
"One inch of wallet equals 9 inches of cock."

A. Marilyn Monroe

B. Hugh Hefner

B. Kim Kardashian

C. Elon Musk

HUGH HEFNER

Gather 'round for the tale of Hugh Marston Hefner (April 9, 1926 – September 27, 2017), the maestro of magazine mischief. This American publishing prodigy didn't just flip through the pages of history; he founded and reigned supreme as the editor-in-chief of Playboy magazine – the go-to glossy for captivating articles and, well, let's just say, eye-catching photography.

Hefner didn't stop at ink and paper. Oh no, he catapulted the Playboy brand into a global galaxy of Playboy Clubs, where the party never ended, and neither did the bunny ears. He lived the high life in opulent mansions, surrounded by the iconic Playboy Playmates, turning every night into a headline-worthy bash.

Beyond the silk pajamas and legendary soirees, Hefner championed some pretty noble causes. He was a staunch defender of First Amendment rights, an animal rescue advocate, and even played a part in restoring the glitz and glamour of the Hollywood Sign.

Love him or loathe him, Hefner was a man of many chapters – some controversial, some commendable, and all undeniably memorable.

MORE!

.der alt man.

gelt vnd gütz gnüg wil ich dir geben . wiltü nach meinem wilen leben. greiff mit d'häd In mein
taschen das schloss wil Ich dir erlasen ₰ DES IVNG WEIB Es hilft Kain schlos vir
frawen list. Kain tre̅w̅ mag sein da lieb nit ist . darumb Ein schlysel der mir gfelt . den wil
ich Kauffen vnd dein gelt ₰ DER IVNG GSEL Ich drag Ein schlosel zu solchen
schlosen . wie wol Es manchen hat verdrosen, der hat der naren Kappen vyll. der
Röcke   lieb Er Kauffen wyl.   Die ungleichen Liebhaber

These are just a few examples of the wide range of unusual paraphilias that exist.
Can you match them with the definitions ?

Acrotomophilia

Eproctophilia

Hybristophilia

Dacryphilia

Somnophilia

Mechanophilia

Formicophilia

Hierophilia

Nasolingus

Oculolinctus

Attraction to machines or inanimate objects, often involving sexual acts with them.

Sexual arousal from insects crawling on the body or being ingested.

Arousal from religious or sacred objects, places, or rituals.

Sexual attraction to or arousal from licking or sucking someone's nose.

A fetish involving licking or sucking another person's eyeballs.

Sexual attraction to amputees or people with missing limbs.

Sexual arousal from flatulence or farting.

Sexual attraction to criminals or those who have committed atrocities.

Sexual pleasure derived from seeing tears or crying.

Arousal from engaging in sexual activities with a sleeping or unconscious person.

1. **Acrotomophilia:** Sexual attraction to amputees or people with missing limbs.
2. **Eproctophilia:** Sexual arousal from flatulence or farting.
3. **Hybristophilia:** Sexual attraction to criminals or those who have committed atrocities.
4. **Dacryphilia:** Sexual pleasure derived from seeing tears or crying.
5. **Somnophilia:** Arousal from engaging in sexual activities with a sleeping or unconscious person.
6. **Mechanophilia:** Attraction to machines or inanimate objects, often involving sexual acts with them.
7. **Formicophilia:** Sexual arousal from insects crawling on the body or being ingested.
8. **Hierophilia:** Arousal from religious or sacred objects, places, or rituals.
9. **Nasolingus:** Sexual attraction to or arousal from licking or sucking someone's nose.
10. **Oculolinctus:** A fetish involving licking or sucking another person's eyeballs.

These are just a few examples of the wide range of unusual paraphilias that exist.

Cleopatra had power and style,
To turn her royal frown
to a smile,
She filled a gourd with mean
bees,
That buzzed' tween her knees
As She was seen coming
up and down the Nile.

Cleopatra
was Born in 69 bc
The last ruler of the Macedonian dynasty
This Sensual and scintillating ballAd
Tells What happened
when she tossed Caesars Salad
Indefatigable no one ,could please her
Since the late roman conqueror Caesar
On Anthony she left her mark
While playing in the dark
She Taught him to titillate And tease her
Her palace was more grand
than that of donald trump
Her booty was more beautiful than j Lo's rump
Many manly mammals
crossed the desert on their camels
But only Anthony Got the hump

Emperor Ai met his end August 1 BC. Before taking his last breath, childless Emperor Ai wished for Dong Xian to inherit his throne, but alas, his counselors had other plans. Swiftly, the Grand Empress Dowager swooped in, snatching the seal of power from Dong Xian's grip and reinstating Wang Mang as the regent. Dong Xian and his spouse were tragically forced to commit suicide.

Emperor Ai wasn't the lone trailblazer in ancient China when it came to having a male companion. Back in the western Han dynasty days (206 BCE to 220 CE), it was quite the trend for emperors to juggle both male companions and wives.

Historian Bret Hinsch spills the tea in "Passions of the Cut Sleeve: The Male Homosexual Tradition in China," claiming that all the ten emperors reigning in the first two centuries of the Han dynasty were proudly "bi," with Ai being the cherry on top. Each ruler had a special male confidant, with their juicy details recorded in the "Records of the Grand Historian" and the "Book of Han."

The Turin Erotic Papyrus is a treasure trove of ancient Egyptian comedy and saucy satire. In one image, we see a woman multitasking like a pro. She's sitting on an ancient pot, pleasuring herself,casually applying lipstick to her lips with a mirror held in her other hand. She engages with an old man nearby.
"You give me nothing, so I have to resort to this!"
"Come here, you dirty criminal!" It seems like he's thoroughly enjoying this moment, as evidenced by his rather, um, enthusiastic display of his hugely erected phallus.

One of the most explicit sex scenes recovered from antiquity.

Max Ziegfeld is a bi-coastal comedian, lyricist, and producer living with severe ADHD .He has opened for Judy Tenuta, Tom Arnold, Michael Longfellow, and many others. He was a medalist (2nd Place) in the 2022 U.S. Comedy Competition and has appeared in NYC's Yaaas Queer Comedy Festival, Burbank Comedy Festival, the World Series of Comedy, and Marty Ingels' Friars' Club Roast. His music video, "BIGFOOT'S LOVE SLAVE", won the 2019 LA Comedy Fest Award for Best Music Video and the 2020 Theatermaker's Song of the Year Award in NYC (original music by Beau Cassidy and directed by Emmy-winner Heather Tom). Max is the creator and lyricist of P*rn AWARDS: THE MUSICAL! — an off-broadway aimed comedy that has appeared on stages in Las Vegas and Los Angeles. A PORN AWARDS concept album, starring Gilbert Gottfried, TONY winners Judy Kaye and Alice Ripley, Judy Tenuta, Garrett Clayton, Christine Pedi, and RuPaul's Drag Race Queen of Queens' Jynkx Monsoon, will be out later this year. Max is one of the producers of the Palm Springs Comedy Festival, where he performs a tribute show honoring the borscht belt comics of vaudeville. Max studied Theatre, Music, and Dance at the Cornish School of the Arts.

MERCHANDISE AVAILABLE
HTTPS://ZIEGFELDSFOLLIES.ETSY.COM
INSTAGRAM
@ZIEGFELDSFOLLIESSTORE
@MAXZIEGFELD

https://linktr.ee/Maxziegfeld

You might also like:
The Jeffrey Dahmer Cookbook
Viagra Blues -Joke Book
Hypochondriacs Hate The Holidays
The Gay Night Before XXXmas
The Three Little Pigs
The Cauldron Spell

Check out all the
Sir Max Ziegfeld Books !

103
HOME
COOKED
MEALS

The Jeffrey Dahmer Cookbook

A collection of hearty and filling recipes

MY BOLOGNE HAD A FIRST NAME

No matter how tough the meat may be, it's going to be tender if you slice it thin enough.
Guy Fieri

Cooking Qoutes from the World's Greatest Celebrity Chefs

CANNIBAL LOVER'S CULLINARY QOUTE BOOK

MAX ZIEGFELD

MAX ZIEGFELD'S

I WANT TO F**KING KILL MYSELF

CARTOONS JOKES

BIGFOOT'S LOVE SLAVE

MAX ZIEGFELD

Max Ziegfeld's
James Blonde
Double OO
He gave you
Stink Finger and Pink Eye
get ready for
Octopussy
COMING IN A THEATRE NEAR YOU !

MAX ZIEGFELD'S
NAPOLEON
I'M A GROWER, NOT A SHOWER.
WHAT SETS HIS BONE APART?

MAX ZIEGFELD'S
HYPOCHONDRIACS HATE CHRISTMAS
Comical Rhyming coloring book

Max Ziegfeld's
Gay
'TWAS, THE NIGHT BEFORE XXXMAS
Get on the Naughty List

MAX ZIEGFELD'S
HYPOCHONDRIACS HATE THE HOLIDAYS
Comical Rhyming Picture Bo for Germaphobes

I'M SO GAY
BEFORE I EAT A PICKLE I SPIT ON IT FIRST

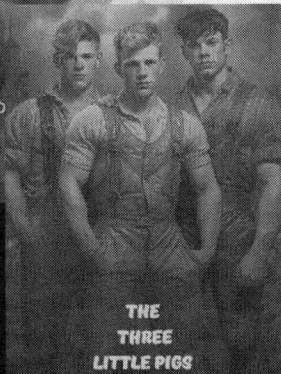

THE THREE LITTLE PIGS
A GAY FAIRY TALE